PENGUIN BOOKS

TALES FROM A PALM COURT

Ronnie Knox Mawer read law at Emmanuel College, Cambridge and after serving in the Royal Artillery was called to the Bar. He went overseas in 1952 and served with HM Overseas Judiciary until 1970. He has now retired from the Bench. He has published many short stories in such magazines as *Punch*, *Cornhill Magazine* and *Argosy*, as well as various papers in legal journals. He and his wife, June, a regular broadcaster with the BBC, divide their time between Wales and London. They have a son and a daughter.

TALES FROM
A PALM COURT

Ronnie Knox Mawer

PENGUIN BOOKS

Penguin Books Ltd, 27 Wrights Lane, London W8 5TZ (Publishing and Editorial)
and Harmondsworth, Middlesex, England (Distribution and Warehouse)
Viking Penguin Inc., 40 West 23rd Street, New York, New York 10010, USA
Penguin Books Australia Ltd, Ringwood, Victoria, Australia
Penguin Books Canada Ltd, 2801 John Street, Markham, Ontario, Canada L3R 1B4
Penguin Books (NZ) Ltd, 182–190 Wairau Road, Auckland 10, New Zealand

First published by Souvenir Press 1986
Published in Penguin Books 1987

Filmset in Palatino
Reproduced, printed and bound in Great Britain by
Hazell Watson & Viney Limited,
Member of the BPCC Group,
Aylesbury, Bucks

Author's Note

Courts of law have one thing in common. For 99 per cent of people, 99 per cent of the time, they are melancholy places.

From the remaining fraction I have collected a few impressions, entertaining ones, I hope. I have thrown them into a hat, altered every name, and written this book.

Contents

1

An Empire Mislaid

'Nothing wrong with you, old boy,' declared Mr Bottomley, the Consultant Physician at the Westminster School of Tropical Medicine.

I had just returned from my first overseas posting, having spent several years on the Bench in what was then British Protected Territory in the Middle East. Mr Bottomley touched a button on the couch and sent me gliding out from behind the screens.

'Not that my students haven't found the range of your complaints most instructive,' he went on. His two young African assistants beamed and nodded as they whisked me upright.

'But you really are one of nature's worriers,' chided Mr Bottomley. He watched me fasten my over-vest. 'It is August, you know.'

'Yes,' I replied, 'the nights are drawing in already.'

The doctor helped me on with my jacket. 'At least I've got you away from all those over-the-counter pills,' he observed. 'Pure hypochondria.'

As he spoke, a tell-tale shower of Windfree Stomach Lozenges cascaded from my inside pocket. I tried to retrieve a few. The consultant peered at me more closely. 'Perhaps you'd pay more attention to what I'm saying if you took that cotton-wool out of your ears!' I began to explain that there was a nasty breeze from the east. 'What is it, sister?' interrupted the doctor. A trim young lady in a blue and white uniform had come into the room.

'Does the Judge still require all these?' she asked, handing him a foolscap sheet. 'The library want to know.'

Mr Bottomley ran his eye down the page. '*The Complete Encyclopaedia of Malarial Diseases*,' he read out. '*The Spleen and its Malfunctions in Equatorial Climates*.' He clicked his tongue. 'Professor Ernst Konberg's *Blackwater Fever—Some Lesser Known Symptoms*.'

'Not that one,' I said. 'I've had it out already.'

'*None* of them, thank you, Sister,' said Mr Bottomley. He tore up the paper and threw it into the wastepaper basket. 'For goodness sake, man,' he exclaimed, 'get your mind off this morbid medical stuff. A good old-fashioned detective yarn and a pint to go with it will do you far more good.'

I pulled on my gloves.

'Anyway,' he concluded at the door, 'you can tell HMG you're perfectly fit. You can be off to the outposts of Empire tomorrow.'

This was more easily said than done. By now the wind of change blowing through the remaining British Colonies had become a hurricane. Harold Langford-Smith (known in the service as Languid-Smith), Appointments Officer at the Dependent Territories Office in Whitehall, made the position quite clear.

'We're almost down to St Helena and the Turks and Caicos Isles,' he pointed out. He opened a drawer in his desk. A mass of papers spilled out. 'Sorry about all this,' he said, 'but at least I don't keep them under the carpet like my predecessor, old Stoddart.' I helped him pick them up. 'Stoddie used to say problems resolve themselves provided they're buried long enough.' The AO rummaged through another drawer.

'Rather think they're after a judge for the Pacific Territories,' he mused. 'Ah!' He seized on a battered file. 'Yes, now I remember,' he said. 'The job was offered to Reggie Parkinson—the judge who had to leave Togoland during the last spot of trouble.' He closed the folder again. 'I understand Reggie is turning it down. Says the South Seas are too far off the beaten track.'

Langford-Smith turned towards the large wall map

behind him, showing the Empire Steamer Routes of 1907.

'Some of the remaining British dependencies are out there, as you probably know.' We studied the map together for a few moments. Eventually the Appointments Officer ringed in a scattering of tiny red dots in the bottom left-hand corner.

'I'd have to confirm the vacancy,' he told me. 'Meanwhile, you might as well take the file and study it for yourself. Conditions of service and so on.' It seemed a good idea, so I left his office with the dog-eared dossier in my briefcase. I caught a bus down to the Law Courts in the Strand.

This was a pilgrimage I always made when in London, rather like a devout Moslem making for Mecca. Those great Victorian-Gothic arches of the Supreme Court of Judicature always reminded me of the famous tag, 'our law is a magnificent edifice'. Of course, as a judge in pretty remote British territories overseas, I only stood guard on the perimeter walls of the edifice, so to speak. Which was why it was important for me to see what was happening on Centre Court from time to time.

I crossed the mosaic tiles and went up the first sweep of stone stairs. The sign at the top, 'Master of the Rolls Court', recalled my earliest appearance as a young barrister. It was before the then President of the Court of Appeal. 'If it please you, my lord, I seek an adjournment', were my first words. They were also my last. My Master in Chambers had arrived to take charge of proceedings. Soon afterwards he suggested I went abroad. So began my career in what, after World War II, Whitehall termed 'HM Overseas Judiciary'.

There were still moments, however, when I wondered whether I might have developed any sort of forensic skill if I had stayed with my contemporaries. Even as I stood at the entrance to the Court of Appeal, I was hailed by one of them—Austin Bulsover, who had been my fellow pupil at the Bar. There he was now, wearing the silk gown of a QC, with an important brief under his arm.

'Long time no see, dear chap!' he exclaimed. 'Still jungle judging, are you?'

'Rather between jungles at present,' I answered.

'Only needs you to set foot in a colony and they're clamouring for independence,' he chortled, in a way I well remembered.

He consulted a slim gold pocket-watch. 'Have to dash. Case in the Family Division. We must lunch in Hall sometime.' He disappeared in a billow of black silk and a whiff of expensive cologne. At his heels trotted Arthur, the elderly Chambers Clerk.

'Doing all right are we, sir?' Arthur asked me. Over his shoulder he confided in a hoarse stage-whisper, 'Fee of yours came in last year. Still waiting for you. One guinea for a bail application—buy you a pair of sun-specs, anyway!'

Bail applications, I thought moving on to the Chancery Court, at least my horizons have widened a bit since then.

In the Chancery Court, the cathedral-like rituals of the Judge's Appearance were in progress—the call for silence by the solemn usher, the rustle as everybody stood while the great man slipped into his throne under the ornate canopy. What chance of a dignified judicial appearance had I ever enjoyed? I pondered, with some envy. Whenever I arrived at Mabasa, on the shores of the Indian Ocean, an excited posse of villagers would splash out to my boat and hoist me on their shoulders.

'Go limp,' the clerk always advised me, as they bundled me ashore like a rugby ball. Even when I was eventually seated in the little mud court-house, my request for silence was invariably drowned by the traditional song of welcome, accompanied by the goat-skin drums of the prison band. True, I was able to accept the usual offering of garlic hung round my neck by the village witch for protection against evil spirits as the equivalent of the mediaeval nosegay presented to judges in England in times of plague. And, with time and patience, I managed a degree of regulation

over the throwing of monkey-nut shells into the well of my
court. But there was no pretending that there was not a
yawning gap between the court in Mabasa and the original
model of English Justice in the Strand. Here, in Chancery,
it was so quiet that you could hear the scratching of the
judge's pen as he made his notes on the argument over the
Trade Marks Act 1938. It was hard to believe that the same
statute had been the cause of a hand-to-hand brawl during
my own sessions four years before.

Ottie Barrack, the local sailmaker, ran a public house at
Al-Jabbah, with Digger Jackson, a retired prospector from
New Guinea, home of the head hunters. They had put up a
sign, 'The Shrunken Head', as the name of their hostelry.
The two men fell out. Each claimed a proprietary right to
this gruesome trade-mark. Ottie opened the proceedings
with a string of abuse. Whereupon Digger crossed the court
and delivered him a swinging right to the jaw.

'You stand committed for contempt,' I warned.

Ottie was no longer standing at all. As they were both
removed from the court, Digger paused in front of me.

'About this trade-mark, Judge,' he said. 'Isn't possession
nine parts of the law?'

'What of it?' I replied.

''Cos the flaming thing's here in me tucker bag,' he
declared. Opening his rucksack he rolled something across
my desk. Mrs Goshi, the stenographer, had never seen a
shrunken head before; she left the room in hysterics. It was
a novel sight for me, too. Oddly enough it flashed through
my mind now, as I stood in the Chancery Division. But at
least His Lordship's lips were seen to move, as he
instructed the clerk to adjourn for the day.

I hurried down to the crypt where the clatter of plates
indicated that the buffet was still open. As I ate my snack, I
took the South Pacific File out of my briefcase. Fresh fields
and pastures new, I thought cheerfully, buttering a scone.
Unfortunately the plastic knife snapped in two. The half
with the butter on it landed in the middle of the papers.

'Could I have a napkin?' I asked the girl behind the coffee-urn.

'You'll have to join the queue again,' she said.

I bent to pick up a two shilling piece, dropped by the lady barrister ahead of me. My fountain pen fell out of my breast-pocket into her plate of baked beans. 'Allow me to pay for another helping,' I insisted.

By the time I got back to my table it had been wiped clean by a jolly West Indian waitress. Too late, I saw the precious South Pacific Papers disappear, with the rest of the litter, down the waste chute in the corner. The situation was irretrievable.

'All gone, daddy-oh,' she explained. 'It's all gone into the crunch-up machine.'

I immediately telephoned the news of my mishap to Langford-Smith. 'You'd better come round,' he said.

Back at the Appointments Office the scene was one of chaos. Every drawer was open, and Langford-Smith's face was serious.

'Bad news, I'm afraid,' he said. I sat down and felt for a Windfree. 'It seems that's the only South Pacific File in existence,' he said.

'But surely . . .' I protested.

Langford-Smith sat behind his desk, his head between his hands.

'Well done,' he said. 'Thanks to you, the remaining British Possessions in the South Pacific have officially ceased to exist!'

2

Settled out of Court

It looked as if my career in HM Overseas Judiciary had ended after a solitary posting. Nostalgically I thought back to my arrival ten years earlier at Sheikh Suliman in British Arabia, where I had been appointed District Judge.

I had left the ship at Jidda and boarded Hadramout Domestic Flight 13—'Mosque Air', as it was called. From the dusty landing-strip, I chartered a desert taxi to the Ali Baba Hotel, Sheikh Suliman, where Government had booked me in. After a late breakfast of rice and mangoes, I obtained directions to the court-house.

This turned out to be the former Army barracks at the far end of the bazaar. The compound had been bombed in 1941, through a mistake by the RAF, but the British Commandant's headquarters at the back had escaped destruction and was now Her Majesty's Court of Justice.

Above the entrance was a sign with one or two missing letters. It read 'DIST - - - T CO - - T. The Union Jack was flying above. At the top of the wooden steps stood a stout man in steel-rimmed spectacles, wearing a crumpled white suit and a red fez. He was flailing the air about him with a large fly-whisk.

'Mr Registrar Bhindi?' I inquired, consulting my letter of introduction.

'Correct,' he snapped.

I proffered a handshake but was obliged to retreat after a painful flick on the nose. The Registrar's intended victim was a cloud of strange insects overhead—rather like prawns with wings.

'Bloody great plague of locusts,' he complained.

After a final sortie on the locusts, Mr Bhindi turned towards the doorway.

'Tipstaff!' he barked.

An elderly Somali, dressed like a beefeater, emerged. I was relieved to see that he was carrying my heavy Robing Box on his head. This all-important sarcophagus, from Ede and Ravenscroft, Chancery Lane, had arrived safely, having been dispatched ahead of me by camel train.

'Follow please,' directed Mr Bhindi.

We arrived at a sort of black hole of Calcutta at the end of the verandah.

'Your Lordship's chambers,' said Mr Bhindi.

He hissed a command in the local dialect. The tipstaff hurried in ahead of us and removed a large mound of clothing from my desk—Mr Bhindi's laundry, long overdue for collection.

The heat inside the chambers was overpowering. I collapsed into a chair, narrowly missing a plate of curried fish, the remains of Mr Bhindi's breakfast. The Registrar aroused a recumbent figure in the corner. 'Punkah Wallah!' he reprimanded. A tattered canvas flap was brought wearily into action overhead.

The tipstaff began to make efforts to open the Robing Box, but the long journey across Arabia's deserts had caused the steel clasps to rust. Fortunately Mr Bhindi produced a scouting-knife and, after a few tense moments, he managed to force the lock.

This, I remember thinking, is how Lord Caernarvon must have felt at the breaching of Tutankhamun's tomb.

The hinges fell apart with a sepulchral groan. I reached inside and drew out what looked like a grey shroud. It was hard to associate this dejected garment with the expensive item listed on the accompanying docket: COURT SHIRT AND JABOT WITH CEREMONIAL TIPPET.

A giant spider abandoned its home in one of the lace cuffs. Mr Bhindi crushed it underfoot with disturbing accuracy.

'Poison sting,' he said, 'narrow bloody squeak.'

I had just got my head through the tail of the shirt when Mr Bhindi's face appeared at the other end.

'Search warrant needed for signature,' he said.

I extricated a hand to sign an authority for the waiting Police Sergeant—to search the Ali Baba Hotel for stolen carpets.

Mr Bhindi consulted the dials of his Japanese gold wrist-watch. 'Time for court,' he announced, opening the door which led from the chambers into the crowded courtroom. 'Silence,' he called.

With the tipstaff's assistance, I struggled into my gown and followed him on to the dais with its sagging green awning.

'Applications!' demanded Mr Bhindi, settling just below me and kicking off his embroidered slippers.

A party of Bedouin shepherds, their bare skins tinged with indigo, came forward. They required a summons against a fraudulent moneylender. Next were three horse-dealers. Their application was to record a contract, ex-changing a white stallion, in the special register kept for that purpose. Mr Bhindi then turned to the criminal matters.

'Fifteen riots,' he proclaimed, handing up a sheaf of charge sheets. I was able to dispose of these fairly rapidly. The prisoners had all escaped over the frontier into Saudi Arabia. We turned to the remainder of the Morning Cause List.

Some of the matters in the list that day, and on the ones that followed, reminded me of courts in England. The smells outside were different—goats, coffee, spices and woodsmoke, instead of fish and chips and petrol fumes—but the pattern of crime was similar: burglaries committed by teenagers, thefts from market stalls committed by women, the equivalent of shoplifting in Britain.

Comparisons like these made the setting a little less strange. And then something would arise that shattered all attempts at familiarisation. Like the Case of the Scuttled Dhow.

It was the Monday of my second week. We had dealt with the Summary Offences—two summonses for reckless speeding against a couple of bullock-cart drivers, and a minor assault upon the Government Tax Collector—when Mr Bhindi moved on to the first of the Formal Indictments.

'Hamid Rashon,' he began, addressing the defendant who had taken his place in the dock, 'you are herein charged with the attempted murder of your grandfather, three uncles, five brothers-in-law and fourteen cousins.'

I looked up in mild astonishment. The prisoner was an amiable-looking young man in a neat white shirt and *futah*.

'How do you answer?' intoned the Registrar.

'Guilty,' came the smiling reply, 'but can explain.'

The courtroom seemed hotter than ever. I wiped my palms on the Imperial Standard Blotter in front of me and asked for the shutters to be opened. A gust of hot air from the Maidan scattered a fine layer of sand over my papers. The sherbert-vendor on the verandah began to drone his invitation for custom.

Mr Bhindi's head surfaced above the edge of the Bench, his jaws moving rhythmically on a large wad of *qat*, the narcotic green leaf that was the chewing gum of Arabia. In between champs, he detailed the particulars of the offence.

'The accused is a partner in the family fishing business,' he recounted. 'On the night in question he and the intended victims were aboard their *dhow* at El Akbar.'

'Where was that?' I asked.

Mr Bhindi searched his pockets for more *qat*. 'In the Al-Jida Straits,' he answered.

He crammed in a fresh mouthful, then paused.

'Would Your Lordship like a chew?'

I shook my head, and Mr Bhindi resumed his account.

'The defendant crept out in the night, opened the drain-cocks, and rowed himself ashore. But within minutes, Lordship,' he declaimed, 'the wind arose, the sail was filled, and the vessel driven safely on a sand-bank.'

'So there were no casualties?' I said.

'And no damage also,' he replied.

I turned to the defendant, who was fingering his prayer-beads, as he leaned over the rail of the dock.

'It was all because my family was cheating me, sir,' the young man began. 'There are many pearls in the Al-Jida Straits. But they take the pearls, leaving me only the oysters.'

'How did you find that out?' I inquired.

'In the market place,' he rejoined, 'where they sold off the pearls. That night I had seen them counting out the monies into my grandfather's turban.' He spread out his hands. 'I suddenly thought I should send them to *El humbra*.'

'The word means Paradise,' explained Mr Bhindi.

At this point, an elderly man with a long hennaed beard stepped forward, holding the tips of his fingers together in greeting.

'I am the grandfather,' he said, 'head of the family.'

He held a brief conference, *sotto voce*, with the Registrar.

'The grandfather says,' reported Mr Bhindi, 'that the family now wish to make this case a matter of compensation only, in accordance with our own Mohammedan Law. The defendant's offer of 5,000 rupees will be accepted. Kindly dismiss the case, my lord, so we can pass on to the next.'

'Out of the question,' I told him sharply. 'This is a British Court. A defendant cannot buy himself out of punishment under English law.'

Mr Bhindi removed his spectacles.

'With respect, my lord, in our country Your Lordship is still a learner-driver.'

'I don't seem to be following you, Mr Registrar,' I observed evenly.

Mr Bhindi reached under the Court Hubble-Bubble for his Works of Reference. After some rummaging, he pushed a tobacco-stained copy of the Criminal Procedure (Territorial Jurisdiction) Ordinance under my nose.

'Your Lordship does not appear to have noticed, from the map on the wall, that the Al-Jida Straits are in the territorial waters of Saudi Arabia. Her Majesty the Queen Elizabeth is not the ruler there, I think.'

'Quite so,' I demurred.

He stabbed a ringed finger onto Section Three of the Ordinance.

'In which case,' he said, 'Mohammedan, not English, law applies.'

There was a round of applause from the back of the court.

'Very well,' I sighed, rising to my feet for some air, 'the case is dismissed.'

Mr Bhindi's bow was unnecessarily low.

'In this case a learner-driver does well to consult the map, my lord,' he murmured, as I withdrew to chambers.

3

Mr Bhindi's Bargain

'What exactly are they doing here?' I remember asking Mr Bhindi one day.

I had come into Sheikh Suliman Domestic Court to find a couple of camels tethered to the witness stand.

'They're mine,' said Mr Bhindi. His steel-rimmed spectacles concealed a remarkably sharp eye for profit and the camels were apparently just another of his bargains.

'Please remove them,' I said, adding with weary irony, 'domestic proceedings are *supposed* to be held in camera.'

Mr Bhindi reluctantly led them to the palm trees beyond the verandah, before summoning the first of the women suitors petitioning my court that morning for a maintenance order.

In domestic cases, Mohammedan, not English, law applied. This was because it was so bound up with the religion of the country, as laid down by the Prophet.

Mohammedan law allowed the husband to divorce his wife merely by saying the word *talak* (I dismiss) three times. The wife, however, had no such right. I was always complaining to Mr Bhindi of the Mohammedan law's unfairness to women and about their lack of compensation, but he would never agree. Dogmatic and intolerant, Mr Bhindi had no sympathy whatsoever for their plight.

'You must not forget the deferred *mahr*,' he always insisted. *Mahr* means dowry. Under Mohammedan law the wife was supposed to get the deferred *mahr* upon divorce. 'The law of *mahr* is all part of the marriage bargain,' he emphasised. 'Thus our Prophet made the law also fair to

women.' Alas for Mr Bhindi! The Mohammedan law of
mahr was to be his downfall.

It was Mr Bhindi's custom in the cool of the day to walk
up the *wadi*, working out his latest profits as he went. He
usually wore a faded Bedouin skirt tightly knotted over his
plump behind and short fat legs. Returning from his walk
one evening, he caught sight of Fatima, daughter of Qadhi
Hassan, unveiled in her father's date garden.

'Of highest value,' he confided to me next morning. 'Like
a pearl from Kuwait.'

I pictured Mr Bhindi restless in his frugal bachelor
retreat. Wakeful at the first glimmer of dawn, he must
have listened distractedly to the *muhsin* calling the faithful
to prayer from the minaret below his house, until Aboker,
the cook, shuffled in with a glass of coffee. This was always,
I knew, an irritating reminder to him of the extravagance
of paying a servant. Sipping his coffee upon one such
morning, Mr Bhindi solved his problem.

'By marrying Fatima, I can do without Aboker,' he
explained to me. I agreed to act as an intermediary to
arrange the marriage. I spoke to Qadhi Hassan upon Mr
Bhindi's behalf. The reply was not unfavourable and we
were invited to call together at the Qadhi's house on the
outskirts of the town. We found the Qadhi sitting over his
books and manuscripts, their ink brown with age. No
mention was made of the purpose of our visit.

A pleasant smell of roasting meat floated over the
verandah. 'Pray eat with us,' said the Qadhi. Cooked rice
was brought in baskets, a table-cloth was laid, dates, bread
and honey were spread upon it. The marriage could not be
discussed until the meal was over. In fact the Qadhi
refrained from mentioning his daughter's *mahr* until we
were leaving.

'It will be but twenty-five camels and 2,000 Marie
Thérèse dollars,' he murmured. 'Out of the question,'
snapped Mr Bhindi. And so, for a while, the matter rested.

It was during the brief rains, when the *wadi* was flooded

with water, that he next saw Fatima. 'She was bathing behind a tamarisk bush,' he recounted. Unfortunately for Mr Bhindi it transpired that Fatima was perfect in figure. He begged me to reopen discussions as to her bride-price.

After considerable bargaining, Mr Bhindi's two camels were accepted as a down payment of *mahr*, with the remainder deferred and to be paid over ten years. They clasped hands.

'There are also the wedding expenses,' the Qadhi hinted. 'Just a ring, candles, sweetmeats, bed and bed coverings. Say two shifts, one of crimson silk, the other of blue cotton; two veils, two pairs of shagreen slippers, four chains for the neck hung with bells, and six gold bracelets. As for the singers and musicians and the cost of the feast—500 dollars at the most.'

Negotiations were again broken off.

Mr Bhindi tried cold baths. He avoided the *wadi*. It was no use. I could see that an unquenchable passion had been aroused in the portly Registrar of Sheikh Suliman Court. Upon his behalf I sent a message to Qadhi Hassan that Mr Bhindi would pay what was demanded.

I witnessed the marriage contract, which the Qadhi sealed with his gold signet ring. The wedding was fixed. It was celebrated on the day after Ramadan and I was privileged to attend.

Mr Bhindi sat on a special mound of carpets, with the Qadhi clicking his rosaries nearby. The hubble-bubble was passed around. Eventually the Qadhi led the way to another room. A latticed door opened onto the bride, cross-legged on the marriage couch. She was encased in rich draperies, her face hidden by veils. Mr Bhindi was placed in the bridegroom's position with the male relations in the opposite corner of the room. The music began. The ensuing feast was lavish and interminable. At last we guests bade the happy couple good-night.

It was traditional among the people of Sheikh Suliman for the bridegroom to take to the marriage-bed first. His clothes had then to be removed by his wife. Custom finally decreed that the bride must resign her veil before extinguishing the light.

I believe it was at this moment that Mr Bhindi let out a stream of unseemly oaths. Seconds later, so the servants told me, his naked and indignant figure streaked across the Qadhi Hassan's courtyard. Mr Bhindi hammered in vain at the Qadhi's door. 'A great fraud, a great fraud,' he cried unheard into the desert air.

Mr Bhindi and the Qadhi were waiting for me when I arrived at court later that morning.

'You have my daughter, Mr Bhindi,' the Qadhi was saying. 'Of what do you complain?'

'Yes,' shrieked Mr Bhindi, 'but which damn daughter—eldest and plainest of the lot!'

The Qadhi laid a soothing hand upon his shoulder, and turned to me. 'I stipulated my daughter,' he answered, 'but not which one.'

Mr Bhindi ground his teeth. 'I will divorce her at once,' he warned. I took out a copy of the marriage contract. 'In that event, Mr Bhindi,' I interposed, 'you must pay the balance of *mahr*—nineteen more camels and 2,000 dollars immediately.'

Mr Bhindi knew he was beaten. With sullen grace he resigned himself to returning to the bridal home. 'All part of the bargain, Mr Bhindi,' I reminded him. 'As you always said, thus the Prophet made the law fair to women.'

That was the only laugh I ever had at Mr Bhindi's expense. More often it was the other way around. In the Overseas Judicial Service, the Court Registrar enjoyed a knowledge of local conditions and language often denied to the Judge. This was an advantage especially savoured by Mr Bhindi.

4

The Perils of Office

'Votch out,' squeaked Mr Tarpawaller, doyen of the local Bar, as I stepped unexpectedly into the Sheikh Suliman Court, on an unforgettable day at the end of Ramadan. An earthenware water-pitcher flew past us. Mr Tarpawaller was the thrower, Mr Bhindi the target.

'Really, gentlemen,' I expostulated. They were known to quarrel, but this was going too far. 'Mr Tarpawaller,' I said, 'despite your venerable age and seniority, I shall have to bind you over if this sort of thing goes on.'

'Flog him,' interjected Mr Bhindi. I motioned the enraged octogenarian back to his seat at the Pleader's Bar. 'Bhindi has refused my application with unforgivable insult,' he quavered. 'Rubbish application,' retorted Mr Bhindi. 'Dead loss contrary to Section 156 Civil Procedure Code.'

Mr Tarpawaller was trying to get to his feet again. 'The learned Registrar has every right to reject an application if procedurally incorrect,' I said.

'But not to stamp his great foot upon it,' complained Mr Tarpawaller. I managed to soothe him down again. 'I shall review the application myself,' I said.

The document of application was still wedged between the thongs of Mr Bhindi's right sandal. He managed to extract it and placed it, somewhat the worse for wear, on the Bench. I had great difficulty in deciphering the unsavoury exhibit.

Mr Tarpawaller was anxious to assist me. 'In my application I am asking Your Honour to review an assessment of rent,' he explained, 'upon one of my own properties.'

'Upon one of his pig-sties,' commented Mr Bhindi.

'I am addressing the Master, not his mule,' said Mr Tarpawaller.

Comparison with the lowest of animals in Arabian tradition was too much for Mr Bhindi's pride. With a gesture of rage he reached up and pushed the punkah in Mr Tarpawaller's direction. Although a gross contempt of court, his action proved no threat to Mr Tarpawaller. The punkah merely rocketed back on its pulleys and took Mr Bhindi with it. In the collision with my desk, my heavy Victorian wig stand shot off sideways and caught me a nasty crack on the knee.

'You're suspended from duty, Mr Bhindi,' I called. Even my nerve had cracked. He hurried out of the courtroom.

Mr Tarpawaller cackled with approval. As I bent to recover a volume of Halsbury from the floor, the words on the open page leaped out at me—'Never sentence in anger.'

I drank a glass of dusty water. 'You can tell Mr Bhindi he may return to work,' I called to the usher who had retreated to the public gallery.

'You'll have to deal with this mess,' I told Mr Bhindi. 'Meanwhile I shall visit the *locus in quo*.'

The *locus in quo*—Mr Tarpawaller's property—was a narrow whitewashed building adjoining the Gardens of Paradise Bottling Factory. It was let as a boarding-house.

'It's the Judge here,' I called through the latticed portico.

The proprietor appeared. He was wearing an army great-coat, an astrakhan hat and an enormous muffler. The shade temperature was 103°F.

'I have to inspect the premises for the purpose of the Rent Act,' I said.

The proprietor looked mystified, but let me in. He understood no English so I tried to explain the reason for my visit by sign language.

'For me to say,' I demonstrated, 'how much *faloos* Landlord Tarpawaller take from you.' I had already picked up a smattering of the language. The proprietor exploded into a violent fit of coughing and tightened up his muffler.

'May as well get on with the inspection,' I decided.

The main reception room had a low wooden platform running along both sides. Six sleeping mats were laid along each platform, providing for twelve inmates. They were presumably out at work.

I noticed a well outside in the courtyard. Water supply was an important factor in assessing rent. 'Water,' I called to the proprietor. 'Is water good?'

He took no notice. He was crouched over a charcoal brazier, groaning and coughing. The poor man was obviously suffering from 'flu. I had, as always, a bottle of aspirins in my briefcase, and handed him two. My action was well meaning, but as it turned out, foolish.

In Sheikh Suliman, a European who produced medicaments from a black briefcase could only be a doctor. The boarding-house proprietor had assumed I was the new Medical Officer on a routine health call. I suppose I should have realised this, but it never occurred to me at the time.

'Has Mr Tarpawaller given you a rent book?' I persisted, making a scribbling gesture on a memo-pad. 'Paper? Landlord give paper?' I repeated. The proprietor downed his tablets and smiled enigmatically. 'Must remember to check that point with Mr Tarpawaller,' I noted.

From the kitchen, where I examined the rather primitive cooking facilities, a circular stone staircase led upstairs. The upper storey was divided into two.

'Quite understand,' I motioned to the proprietor when we reached a curtained partition on the second floor. 'Purdah quarters beyond here. Wouldn't dream of going in.'

To my surprise, he took me by the arm and insisted upon my entering. He spoke quietly to the veiled lady within.

'Not essential,' I said, making a quick check of the room's dimensions, 'but thank you all the same.' I was about to go, when to my astonishment the lady began to pull up her dress.

Good God, I thought, had I blundered into some sort of
house of ill fame?

Her husband, the boarding-house keeper, smiled approvingly as she exposed a plump knee for my inspection.
She further startled me by rubbing her hand over her
knee and groaning. It was then that I noticed that the limb
was swollen. Her husband pointed to the contused joint.

'Him broke?' he demanded. 'Gracious me,' I exclaimed as
the truth dawned. Believing that I was the Government
Doctor on a public health visit, both husband and wife
wished me to examine the lady's injured leg.

Just then I recognised a familiar voice on the terrace
beyond the curtains. It was one of the few occasions when I
was glad to hear that Mr Bhindi had arrived. Advocate
Tarpawaller was with him. I hurriedly joined them.

'Have you gentlemen cleared up your misunderstanding?'
I asked. They nodded. 'Then you'd better clear up this one,'
I said.

Mr Bhindi proceeded to interpret the true reason for my
visit. Upon learning that she had exposed herself to a
Nazarene stranger who was not the Government Doctor
at all, the proprietor's wife affected hysteria. Her wailing
was taken up by all the other female inhabitants of the
purdah quarter.

'For heaven's sake Mr Bhindi,' I urged, 'tell them nobody
regrets the mistake more than myself. And they can count
upon me for a very fair assessment of rent when I leave.'
Mr Tarpawaller beckoned me to a peep-hole in the
verandah parapet. From there I could see that a crowd had
gathered below. They were obviously in a very nasty
mood.

'Maybe Your Honour vill not be leaving,' he piped. It
seemed that an ugly distortion of the incident had spread
around the bazaar.

'Side exit,' signalled Mr Bhindi. He popped a lady's black
purdah-cloak over my head and led me down some back
stairs.

'Where are you taking me?' I whispered, stumbling forward into some sort of carriage, heavy with the scent of jasmine.

'It's the back seat of my motor-car,' hissed Mr Bhindi, 'where I usually hide my wife.' He drew across the dividing curtain and drove me undetected through the hostile throng. To them, at that moment, I was a sex-maddened infidel who had tricked his way into the women's quarters of the boarding house.

'Quick thinking on your part,' I congratulated him when he delivered me safely home. He was about to return to the bazaar to explain to the populace the truth of the situation.

'Perhaps now we hear less from Your Honour about emancipation of women,' observed Mr Bhindi.

5

On Probation

'I'm not sure about these howling dervishes,' I said to Mr
Tarpawaller, upon his next appearance before my court.
'How far would they respond to probation?'

Mr Tarpawaller's clients, a splinter group of this
extreme religious sect, had contravened the Public Order
Regulations in Sheikh Suliman.

'Vell,' insisted Mr Tarpawaller, 'being first offenders,
they all come under the Probation Act.' As he spoke, the
leader of the defendants threw his black coat down into the
well of the court and leaped several feet into the air.
'Yahoo,' he called in my direction.

'He is feeling great religious joy,' explained Mr
Tarpawaller.

'I'd rather he didn't,' I said. 'This is a court of law, not a
mosque.' 'Yahoo,' repeated the leader with another disturbing leap.

'Ya-Hoo is Arabic,' Mr Tarpawaller continued. 'It means
"O Great Power".'

'Tell him I have no wish to be addressed in that way,' I
instructed Mr Tarpawaller.

I turned to the court usher. 'See if the learned Registrar
has finished his lunch,' I said.

The duties of Probation Officer at Sheikh Suliman were
performed by Mr Bhindi. It was yet another title he had
added to his list of Court Registrar, Official Receiver,
Public Trustee, Registrar of Births and Deaths, Commissioner for Oaths, Under-Sheriff, Assistant Master of
the Court of Protection and Administrator of Wrecks.

'It seems, Mr Bhindi,' I explained to him when he

appeared, 'I've no choice but to place these gentlemen on probation.'

Mr Bhindi reluctantly put away his tooth-pick. 'Up to you,' he said. He prodded the defendants to their feet with the carved ebony stick he had acquired upon a trading visit to East Africa. As one man, the fanatical pack sprang into the dock. For an instant I feared they were about to break into their infamous 'whirling dance'.

'I am placing you on probation,' I announced. 'The court will keep a close check on your progress.' Mr Bhindi marshalled them away.

From the verandah a kind of banshee howl died away: 'Yahoo, Yahoo, Yahoo . . .'

'Mad people is holy,' observed the usher. I tried to imagine our stout padre spinning and howling up the aisle.

'Not in the Anglican community,' I replied.

It was three months later when Mr Bhindi reminded me of certain duties towards the dervishes.

'You are required to visit their place of abode,' he pointed out. He opened his copy of Hodgkin on *Probation of Offenders* and shook out the termites. The preface to Hodgkin contained a photograph of a Mr Nelson, the first probation officer in the world, appointed at Bow Street Court in 1876. Mr Nelson wore a frock-coat and a clerical collar. Mr Bhindi studied the photograph carefully.

'Where are the dervishes living at present?' I inquired. Mr Bhindi closed the book with a sigh. He hankered after the dignity of Mr Nelson's frock-coat and clerical collar.

'They are camping on the oasis at Malabar,' he told me. Malabar lay in the desert far away from any roads.

'Hardly on the bus route,' I chaffed.

Mr Bhindi polished his spectacles impassively. 'We go there by camel,' he announced.

During the days of preparation that followed, I had moments of apprehension. True, I reminded myself, my predecessors in mediaeval times, the assize judges, had travelled the English countryside on horseback. But my own experience with horses had not given me confidence. Two weeks after I was conscripted, during the war, into the Royal Horse Artillery, my steed had slowed down my army career by throwing me over a gun carriage. Camels, I told myself, are more placid than horses.

'Placid' was not altogether the word to describe the obstreperous beast chosen by Mr Bhindi for my own particular use.

'Tip-top,' Mr Bhindi assured me, 'with strong head-stall on.' After a brief struggle, my camel was safely harnessed into a squatting position.

'All ready,' said the court usher.

The *al-shada*, or camel saddle, has a front and rear pommel of tamarisk wood. Between the pommels a sheepskin cushion fits snugly over the hump.

'Very comfortable,' I said, once I had my knees into gear on either side. However, one's sense of judicial isolation, as it were, was alarmingly increased when the camel stood up. 'Hold on,' I called, peering down from what by any standard was a dizzy height, 'there must be a camel with shorter legs than this one.'

'Pull the rope to the left of the neck,' said Mr Bhindi. I did so and the camel lurched forward. 'It's no good,' I called, 'there's simply nothing whatsoever to hold on to up here.'

With the aid of several policemen and the Court staff I managed to get safely to earth. It was obvious that some alternative must be devised. 'I am having Your Honour's camel fitted with a *Dhalla*,' Mr Bhindi decided.

The *Dhalla* turned out to be an elaborate travelling litter made of Berber sheepskins slung from poles across the camel's back. It had protective screens of basketwork on either side.

'Much more sensible,' I approved, safely installed behind the great winged contraption. Mr Bhindi supervised the attachment of my lead rein to the harness of his own beast.

'*Dhalla* used only by women and children,' he said as we set off. I could sense his disapproval, even from twenty feet behind him. But at least we were progressing safely and in some dignity.

The loping rhythm of the camel's tread was unexpectedly soothing. It was as though I were being wheeled along in a giant perambulator. I dozed off.

Night was upon us by the time we reached Malabar. A shrouded figure in a white head-cloth emerged from under an olive tree.

'*Salaam aleikhum,*' he greeted me. It was the dervish leader. His beard had grown at least six inches and seemed to crackle with a life of its own. He took me by the arm. Goodwill was intended but I could not repress an involuntary yelp as his hawk-like talons sank into my elbow. He nodded with a smile and echoed my exclamation.

'He, too, is hungry,' translated Mr Bhindi.

Before the camp fire a frugal supper was laid. Fellow dervishes exploded from the surrounding tents, each carrying a lighted taper. We all sat down to eat. 'Sorry no meat,' interpreted Mr Bhindi, on behalf of our host. 'The last sheep have strayed into desert and camel too valuable.'

'But this is good,' I demurred, dipping into the bowl of whitish gravy before me. Under Mr Bhindi's scowl I hastily swapped over to my right hand. I never could remember which one was forbidden for eating, by Koranic custom. 'What food is it?'

'Sour camel milk,' explained the leader. 'It is called curds.'

'Ah—curds and whey!' I exclaimed.

The tribal story-teller had been entertaining us with dervish folk-tales. I felt it was my turn to respond. I was free to do so without making an ass of myself since Mr Bhindi had gone to supervise the sleeping arrangements.

'Little Miss Muffet,' I began, seized by the inspiration of the moment, 'sat on a tuffet, eating her curds and whey.' In my elation I performed a quick charade, utilising my travelling camp-stool and one of the milk bowls. 'There came a big spider,' I went on, gathering momentum, 'that sat down beside her, and frightened Miss Muffet away.' At

the climactic moment my start of feigned horror was
almost too real. Mr Bhindi had returned out of the shadows
and was squatting behind me. His beady eye swivelled onto
me.

'One over the seven, maybe?' he whispered.

'What, on camel's milk?' I giggled. He steadied me as I
skidded on a squashed date.

'Dervish curds are always fermented,' he replied. 'Go to
head like alcohol.'

I acknowledged the grunts of appreciation from around
the fire as I made my exit. Inside my tent, Mr Bhindi tucked
my travelling blanket snugly about me. My head was whirling. 'Dam' dervishes,' I murmured, sinking into oblivion.

The next thing I knew was Mr Bhindi's face at the tent-
hole, the sunshine blinding behind him. 'Hanging over,
sir?' he gloated.

'Nothing that a Livingstone Rouser won't put right,' I
countered. It was a large pill that only went down when
combined with a heavy draught of magnesia. I had learnt
never to stir from base without my canvas medical
holdall—a purchase from the Tropical Outfitters in London.

Mr Bhindi was doubling up as chambermaid this morning.
He handed me a bowl of brackish water and supervised my
ablutions watchfully. I sometimes felt I was the object of
some anthropological study Mr Bhindi was compiling on
the Customs and Habits of the British Male in Desert
Conditions.

'These dervishes,' I began, as I started to shave. I turned
away to conceal an unaccountable tick that had developed
overnight below my left eye. But the mirror in Mr Bhindi's
hand followed me remorselessly.

'Yes, sir?'

'It's no use pretending that I understand their ecumenical
outlook,' I continued. I dipped unobtrusively into the
Rousers again. 'But now they've settled quietly on their
own out here, they seem to be harming no one.'

'No one?' hinted Mr Bhindi.

'Impartiality is the hallmark of English justice,' I reminded him. 'I would never allow my personal indisposition or feelings to mar its proper course.'

I threw the soapy water out of the tent, missing Mr Bhindi by a few well-judged inches. 'I have decided to free the dervishes from all restrictions under the Probation Act,' I told him.

Mr Bhindi, who was still consuming the remains of his breakfast, disposed of a handful of walnut shells into my sandals. 'Your Honour should not do that,' he insisted. 'These men cannot be trusted.'

'Nonsense,' I answered. 'The probation order will be discharged in this case when I return to Sheikh Suliman.'

Further disapproval from Mr Bhindi was cut short by a call from outside. My own breakfast, it seemed, was awaiting me. 'Kindly ensure our camels are harnessed and ready,' I instructed the Registrar.

I followed the dervish leader to where my own meal was laid out. A spicy aroma met me from the cooking-pot on the fire. It smelt this time like a non-vegetarian menu. 'For the Judge,' said the dervish leader.

Onto my banana leaf he ladled—clearly in my special honour—a succulent portion of braised liver. 'Return of the lost sheep?!' I exclaimed, tucking in. My host chuckled into his beard. A man with a sense of humour, I approved, despite the barriers of creed and custom.

I had almost finished the dish when Mr Bhindi appeared at my shoulder.

'Our camels ready, Mr Bhindi?' I inquired.

'Mine is,' he replied. He wore a more than usually smug expression.

'And mine?'

Mr Bhindi pointed a finger at the last fragment of meat on my dish. 'Nice and tender?' he inquired. I nodded, mystified.

'Younger camel make best feast,' declared Mr Bhindi. 'Taken, slaughtered, cooked—while we sleep!'

I listened dumbfounded while Mr Bhindi went on to explain that he had just seen the dervishes butchering the remainder of my camel behind the encampment.

A dervish elder interrupted Mr Bhindi's accusations and began an impassioned speech. 'He is saying Your Honour's camel wandered in the night and fell to its death down the ravine.'

'Does he mean that four-foot gully we crossed on our way to the oasis?' I asked. Mr Bhindi nodded. 'A gross theft of the meanest kind,' I burst out. 'Tell these scoundrels that no one will go unpunished!'

Mr Bhindi drew me to one side. 'Maybe Your Honour is now forgetting hallmark of English justice,' he chided. 'Angry suspicion is no proof.'

Our sole remaining means of transport was chewing contentedly in the background. I was scrambling aboard behind Mr Bhindi when he turned towards me.

'Is Your Honour still planning to discharge their Probation Order for good conduct?' he dared to inquire.

The dervishes parted ranks to let us through. Their leader bowed an impertinent farewell.

'It is reminding me of old Arab proverb,' called Mr Bhindi over his shoulder, as we set off on the return journey to Sheikh Suliman. 'The wise man who steals a traveller's beast invites him to the meal.'

It was checkmate to Mr Bhindi.

6

Tennis with the Sultan

Malakar is a rocky isthmus off the Gulf of Alkazir. It was
visited in turn by the Abyssinians, the Malays, the
Persians, the Portuguese, the Spanish, the Dutch, the
French, the Turks, the Germans and the British. All were
stunned by its repulsive aspect save the British, who built a
coaling station there in 1869. The proprietors, Eastern
Shipping Ltd of London, had bought the site from Omar
IV, Sultan of Malakar, in return for a large consignment of
arms.

In 1934 the coaling station closed down. For twenty
years Malakar lay deserted. Then oil was discovered under
its crumbling wharves.

'My reward from the Holy Prophet,' claimed the reigning
Sultan, Omar V, who had recently endowed a new mosque
for the Malakar sultanate. The local representative for
Eastern Shipping Ltd disagreed.

Litigation began in the Supreme Court of British Arabia.
The Senior Judicial Commissioner was away on leave and I
was taking his place for the first time.

There was another reason for my feeling apprehensive
about the occasion. I was not permitted my familiar court
setting with its homely, if raucous atmosphere. Under the
Judicial Encampment (Mesopotamia, Persian Gulf and
Southern Arabia) Regulations (1921), the summer session
of the Supreme Court was held in a large Durbar tent. This
was fashioned, I was told by Mr Bhindi, who accompanied
me, upon the one used by George V, King Emperor, when
he received the homage of the Indian Princes at Delhi on 12
December 1911. I was to preside from the central dais, wear-

ing a light wig rather than the Imperial Crown of India.

The weather on the fateful day turned out to be
changeable. I was waiting in the wings for a signal from Mr
Bhindi, who was laying out the papers on my desk.

'Better slacken off those guy-ropes,' I whispered to him.

The *shamal*—a sudden gust of desert wind—had blown
up, causing the marquee to billow and sag. I was reminded
of a childhood visit to Bertram Mills' circus when a
thunderstorm had broken out. I had always been a timid
child and had had to be taken out to be sick.

Fortunately for my nerves on this occasion, the *shamal*
died away as quickly as it had come, and danger seemed to
have been averted. A faint sigh of disappointment went up
from the waiting crowd as I took my place unharmed on the
platform. Better things awaited them, however. The next
moment the entrance flaps to the arena were drawn apart
with a flourish. A burly figure, magnificent in black *aba* and
golden *burnous*, made his appearance, and all heads were
bowed.

'His Highness the Sultan of Malakar,' announced Mr
Bhindi.

I beckoned the Sultan forward to a cane chair in the
witness stand. His young attendant slipped an embroidered
cushion under the ruler's feet. He took the oath with a
twinkle in his eye. Several large rings flashed as he settled
his robes and smoothed his short black beard.

'My father,' the Sultan began in evidence, speaking
perfect English, 'allowed the shipping company to use
Malakar for their coaling station. It was a favour, nothing
more.'

'But unfortunately, Your Highness,' I pointed out, 'the
deed signed by your illustrious ancestor says otherwise.' I
extricated the conveyance from the company file.

'It says that he was paid for the sale of the land and all
that lay beneath it.'

The bland smile remained on the Sultan's plump face. He
shook his head quietly.

'His Highness's father,' interjected Mr Bhindi, 'never cut his beard.'

'I don't see what that's got to do with the case,' I rejoined.

Mr Bhindi let forth one of his groans of disapproval at my stupidity. 'In Malakar it is a sign of perfect wisdom,' he lectured. 'Would such a great man part with all rights in family land?'

I was studying the conveyance again when there was a disturbance at the back of the court. A group of indigo-painted Bedouin pressed forward, clutching rifles to their naked chests.

'The Sultan's bodyguard,' explained Mr Bhindi. 'They say they must stand between you and His Highness.'

'Certainly,' I agreed, 'provided they surrender their weapons.'

Twenty Mauser rifles clattered onto my desk.

I turned my attention back to the deed of conveyance.

'Your Highness cannot dispute the clear wording and the signature,' I said. I leaned forward and tried to pass over the document but the hand of the commander of the bodyguard intervened. Eventually the document reached the Sultan.

'Does Your Highness not agree it is your father's signature?' I asked.

The Sultan purported to have forgotten his reading glasses and merely waved it away. The red-turbaned commander handed it back to me. When I bent to re-examine it, I myself had difficulty in deciphering the vital words. I clicked my tongue irritably. The indigo thumb-marks would undoubtedly cause problems for any court of appeal. It was lucky I had been able to read the document first.

'I'm afraid my ruling must be against Your Highness,' I announced.

The crowd rustled with interest. Someone threw a mango at me but missed.

The Sultan rose and gathered his cloak about him. He seemed to accept the decision without demur. Mr Bhindi, on the other hand, chose this moment to behave with disgraceful partiality.

'Your Honour make bad mistake,' he breathed, behind his hand.

I made a mental note to inquire at the next opportunity as to his business interests in the Sultan's name.

As His Highness swept off, Mr Bhindi led the way out backwards, bending ever lower in the process. He had reckoned, though, without a hole in the matting, and his obsequious charade terminated with an impromptu backwards somersault.

'Mr Bhindi,' I said, 'this is not the Big Top. Nor are you expected to give a performance as Coco the Clown.'

Even the iron control of justice can sometimes break.

'Karate training,' Mr Bhindi replied. 'Come in handy! I teach you sometime.'

He sealed my judgement against the Sultan with sulky reluctance, and my brief session in the Arabian Supreme Court was concluded.

However, that was not my final meeting with the losing side in the case. 'Let us try our court this time,' read the message I received, an invitation from the Sultan to a game of tennis at his palace. I was on local leave at the time. The up-country Government Resthouse, where I was staying, lay in the hills adjoining his residence.

At the palace, liveried bearers conducted me through the marble colonnade. The Sultan, dressed, this time, in a white *aba* and *burnous*, welcomed me with great charm.

'The sun will get very hot,' he warned. 'Headgear is essential.' He handed me a large American base-ball cap, which came down over my ears.

The Sultan took my hand and pointed in the direction of the tennis court. We came to a junction in the path. I was about to lead on through an arched trellis-way covered in jasmine. His Highness's hand on my shoulder brought me back.

'Not that way,' he smiled. 'I don't imagine the ladies of

my household would be quite up to a mixed doubles.'

A tinkle of merry laughter came from the latticework beyond. I was aware of several pairs of hidden eyes following my retreating back.

We took up positions on the sandy court.

'May Allah give thee wings,' announced my opponent from the other end. His remark was addressed, in Arabic, at the tennis ball, which he served at me, underarm and without warning.

'Fifteen points,' claimed the Sultan, adjusting his *burnous*.

I began to protest. There was a warning click from a rifle bolt behind some oleander bushes. I caught a glimpse of a familiar red turban. It was the commander of the bodyguard. I lost the game.

We changed ends and my first service began to go in. There was a flurry of sand and His Highness missed a return. It was the first time I had seen him lose his silky composure.

'Burn it into ashes,' he shouted, casting the racquet aside, narrowly missing his private secretary, a scholarly-looking man in spectacles, who was watching anxiously on the side line. Two ball-boys scurried forward, laden with new racquets.

The Sultan's next drive hit the top of the net and fell back. To my astonishment, he drew a gold *jambia* from his waist and struck at the net.

'I have destroyed an evil *jin*,' he explained, with a wry smile.

We were soon hard at it again. 'Like the sun,' quipped the Sultan, 'there is much fire in me.' A long rally followed which His Highness won.

The senior ball-boy took advantage of the interval when we changed ends to sprinkle his master with rose-water, while I was offered a glass of lime. The Sultan made a careful examination of his side of the court. A tiny furrow was detected. He summoned another minion and a small donkey was led out with a log roller to put this right.

Revived again, His Highness ordered play to recommence. Pounding heavily to and fro, he made a close game of it. Eventually I neared match point.

'Stop,' requested the Sultan, dropping his racquet and turning towards Mecca. High up in a minaret of the palace mosque, the holy man was calling the faithful to prayer. This time a procession of retainers filed onto the court bearing hand-bowls, towels and prayer mats.

'Now,' said His Highness, rising in due course from his devotions, 'I feel the strength of twenty Bedouin.' Like a Wimbledon champion, he began smashing balls away. I started to lose points. 'Ah,' he called, 'the victory is slipping through your fingers like sand.' Unnerved, I surrendered the match.

We rested upon a pile of carpets on the verandah where the air was rich with incense.

'So much depends,' beamed the Sultan, handing me a juicy segment of water melon, 'upon one's choice of courts.'

My loss of the match was already known to Mr Bhindi when I returned to work after the holiday.

'About this fellow you call Coco the Clown,' he said, as he stepped in front of me to open the door that led on to the Bench.

'What about him?' I asked.

'Maybe he plays tennis like Your Honour,' chuckled the Registrar.

I made no reply.

7

Days of Challenge

'I'm God,' snapped the defendant in answer to the charge of common assault.

'Then no doubt you'll be pleading not guilty,' I observed. Mr Bhindi said nothing.

The defendant wore a red beard and a blanket. He settled back in the dock with Olympian detachment as the evidence against him was called.

It transpired that he had been distributing private tracts outside the Mosque. He claimed to be the New Messiah. The complainant, a devout fisherman, had challenged this assertion. The defendant assaulted the fisherman. Hence the proceedings before me.

'Does the accused wish to give testimony on—er—divine oath?' I inquired of Mr Bhindi.

'Certainly not,' he replied.

I bound the Almighty over. He shook hands all round and departed, after appropriating, we afterwards discovered, the court copy of the Bible.

The remaining cases from the bazaar that day were more humdrum; the usual bevy of stall-holders sued for debt.

The debtors' prison was a little shuttered house on the outskirts of the settlement. It was run by an enterprising lodging-house keeper. The cost of boarding the inmates had to be met by the creditors themselves.

'Why, Mr Yahooda,' I once asked a prosperous money-lender, 'do you insist upon the defendant's going to prison?' I suggested that he would find it cheaper to allow his debtor to carry on working. 'At least he might earn something to repay you,' I pointed out.

Mr Yahooda was adamant. He made away with his client to the debtors' prison.

Back came Mr Yahooda a few weeks later asking for the prisoner to be released. 'That riff-raff fellow,' he sobbed, 'his belly's got so fat on rice I am paying for, he now ask for new clothes to fit him!' Mr Yahooda would have welcomed the law of Ancient Rome which permitted a creditor to cut out a piece of the debtor's stomach.

The construction of a vast new oil refinery across the estuary from Sheikh Suliman gave me a busy time as judge of the Workmen's Compensation Court. Abdulla, a Yemeni tribesman, who had come across the desert frontier to sign on for the construction company, would injure himself at work. The tariff of compensation under our Workmen's Compensation Act—say 500 rupees for the loss of Abdulla's little finger—was a system widely recognised by many ancient laws. In AD 605 King Ethelbert awarded three shillings for the loss of a thumb-nail. I had always been irritated by King Ine of Wessex, AD 700. For knocking off a Welsh or Scots man he prescribed half the compensation given for killing a Saxon. King Alfred preferred to distinguish between the sexes. He ordered twice the amount for violence to a man as he did for violence to a woman.

Mr Bhindi would have agreed with King Alfred. So would most of the male community in Sheikh Suliman.

'Why,' I demanded one afternoon of Ali, a mild little watchmaker from the Suk, 'did you beat your wife?'

'Because she went to the football match,' he answered. The explanation struck me as inadequate.

'Well,' came the patient explanation through the interpreter, 'all the other women who went with her have been punished by their husbands. Many have also been divorced, but I have been merciful.'

A popular team of Egyptian footballers had visited the town. Some of the more intrepid wives had ventured from their purdah quarters to peep at the game. Caught *in flagrante delicto* they had been severely dealt with by outraged husbands. Unfortunately, Ali had been seen setting about his spouse by a government official. This led to his appearance in court and a sharp fine.

The punishment of the lady football fans reminded me of a law of Ancient Greece. Any woman who crossed the Alpheus to watch the Olympic Games was to be thrown from the top of Mount Typhaion.

Games, or rather gaming, in the non-Olympian sense, was something else which we tried to control overseas, just as in England. Hence the occasion when I tried 134 Chinamen for gaming. Nobody in the Chinese dockland community could understand why. The game was called *Fan Tan*. They had always played it. 'Why,' they asked themselves, 'should English law forbid it?' However, under the English Gaming Acts, such games of chance were illegal. It was unusual to see any Chinaman in a criminal court, for the Chinese minority was law-abiding. There was no room for the public at the hearing because the defendants filled every nook and cranny.

'A lidiculous tlial,' commented Mr Li Po Lung, defendant number forty-nine, leaping to his tiny feet from his seat upstairs in the gallery. Mr Lung was a restaurant proprietor, respectable and well liked. The evidence against Mr Lung and his 133 companions was clear. They had been playing *Fan Tan* and so I had to collect 655 rupees from them. They paid up dutifully, but Mr Lung was by no means the first to question the suitability of certain English laws which we introduced overseas.

The basics of English law and order, the system of courts, our traditions of justice, were not unwelcome. What was queried was the wholesale reception of English law into such different societies. A light meal of the laws of England might be a good thing. It was the seven-course dinner which caused indigestion.

Indigestion, or worse, food-poisoning, was a major issue in a case I tried a year or two later. Mr Hak, owner of the

Crescent Night Club, was summonsed under the Public Health Regulations for serving meals from unhygienic kitchens.

'Filthy lies,' he insisted when the charges were put.

'The court will see for itself,' I announced and adjourned the hearing.

At the suggestion of the Public Health Inspector I paid a surprise visit to the club in the evening.

The lights were all out at the Crescent Night Club when I arrived. Policemen tussled with an angry crowd of seamen outside.

Most ships bound for the East fuelled at the harbour nearby, so Mr Hak's establishment was popular with sailors of many nationalities or, rather, unpopular on this occasion. The target for their displeasure was Mr Hak, prominent in an off-white dinner jacket.

'Everybody hold horses,' he implored from behind the entrance kiosk. 'Lighting plant gone for the burton,' he confided, smuggling me through a side entrance to a seat near the band.

It was some time before I realised that a shortish lady was peeping at me over the table.

'My wife is saying, "how's tricks",' explained Mr Hak, introducing his other half, or, more accurately, his other quarter. 'Kindly dance her,' decreed my host. Mohammed Abdulla bin Hassam and his Crescent Seven were playing 'Moonglow' as we took to the floor.

Somebody knocked over a hurricane lamp. 'Are you there, Mrs Hak?' I called, having lost her underfoot during the samba.

The electricity came on again. Twelve o'clock came, and with it the cabaret.

'Shufti, my lord,' whispered Mr Hak. 'Shufti my daughters.' He indicated two ladies of the chorus, whose sinister features I had thought familiar. 'They are learning since the cradle,' he said.

Just then the cook emerged from the distinctly whiffy

kitchens. 'Give the big hand,' directed Mr Hak. The enterprising menial began a juggling display.

'He'd do well on the British halls,' I murmured politely.

'We are loving everything British,' enthused Mr Hak, already excessively drunk. 'Steady there, Mr Hak,' I remonstrated. He had me in a damp embrace.

'I am loving you, my lord, like a blood brother,' Mr Hak persisted. 'Like a bloody brother,' he emphasised with rare affection.

During the enforced absence of the chef, a curry caught alight in the rear annexe. I managed to escape amid the excitement.

The fire obliged Mr Hak to rebuild his kitchens, so I deferred sentence in the case against him to make sure that the new premises and equipment satisfied the Health Inspector.

This also allowed me to forget about Mr Hak for the time being and get on with the many other cases awaiting attention. For in this way at least, court in Arabia was no different from the United Kingdom. The backlog of cases was always on the increase.

'Will you adjourn for lunch?' I recall my neighbour enquiring as I set forth for another busy session. 'Not a hope,' I replied. 'There is bound to be a heavy list.'

I remember that I was able to deal fairly smartly, for one reason or another, with the remands that day. I then embarked upon the first of the trials.

Two Yemeni carpet-dealers were charged with illegal possession of a home-made firearm. A cheerful policeman from the border police station produced the firearm.

Mr Tarpawaller rose shakily to cross-examine. 'Vell,' he said, 'vill it shoot?' The happy policeman looked sad. 'Answer the question. Make for him to answer my question,' insisted Mr Tarpawaller.

'I cannot know, sir, I have not fired it,' said the policeman.

Mr Tarpawaller threw up his hands. There was a wheezing sound from his throat. Without a word he bowed himself out on to the verandah. He spat into the dust and bowed himself back into court.

'Submission, Your Honour,' he croaked. 'No case to answer, Your Honour, sir.'

Mr Tarpawaller sat down. 'Just a moment, Mr Tarpawaller,' I said, taking up the firearm. 'This is obviously a trigger.'

It was not so much the deafening sound when it went off as the gaping hole in the roof which disconcerted me. 'A convenient time to adjourn,' I muttered through the swirling dust.

'So,' said my neighbour, a little later, 'you did adjourn for lunch.'

'Not for lunch, just for brandy,' I replied.

8

In the Chair

'Sorry about the late start,' I apologised to Mr Bhindi one day. I was not usually unpunctual, but a sandstorm had delayed my arrival at court.

The Registrar lifted his fez, bowed curtly and began to rattle through the day's cases at an impossible speed.

'Drunk in charge of a Donkey Cart Contrary to Section Sixty-seven of Traffic Act, Watering Goat Milk for Sale Contrary to Section Fourteen of Food Act, Desecration of Holy Tomb Contrary to Section Thirty-eight Burial Laws Amendment Act, Counterfeiting Marie Thérèse Dollars Contrary to Coining Act, Beating Carpets in the Street Punishable under Street Offenders Act, Theft of Water Contrary to Irrigation Regulations Schedule Two.' He paused for breath. The dock was now jammed with defendants.

Mr Bhindi stabbed a podgy forefinger in the direction of the inebriated muleteer. 'Guilty or Not Guilty?' he demanded.

There followed a heated exchange in Arabic. 'He says he's not guilty,' reported Mr Bhindi. The defendant hiccupped alarmingly.

'Perhaps he hasn't understood you, Mr Bhindi,' I said. The Registrar shook his head.

'Well, it's exceedingly difficult even for me to follow you,' I complained. 'And for my part,' I added with a touch of asperity, 'I'm as sober as a judge.'

As I spoke, the defendant fell back into the arms of the court usher. We put his case back until the end of the day; this at least meant he could sleep off the disastrous effects of his toddy-drinking in the cells.

I fined the fraudulent milkman, and began the hearing of

the Burial Act offence. The accused was a wandering Yafei musician, clad in a shabby white chemise with a sash of threadbare red velvet across his right shoulder.

'Arrested while cooking his supper on the tomb of Saint Sayid Hashid,' declared Mr Bhindi.

The musician sucked mournfully on an empty tobacco pipe, fashioned out of a used cartridge shell.

'How could he tell it was a tomb?' I inquired. 'Everybody knows that,' said Mr Bhindi. 'I ought to see for myself,' I persisted.

I adjourned to look at the site. This meant a ten-minute walk in the broiling sun. The tomb was on the very edge of the township, partially hidden under a tuft of wild palms. We pitched an informal camp in the meagre shade.

I turned to speak to the defendant. He was about to take a quiet nap against a sand dune.

'Did you come here by night?' I asked. The old musician nodded. 'I suppose we could return at sunset,' I began, then caught sight of the expression on Mr Bhindi's face.

I moved away to examine the cairn of limestone. I was pretty certain in darkness no visitor could have recognised it for what it was. 'Case dismissed,' I ruled.

'And the blessings of Saint Sayid will follow you all your days,' decared the old man.

There was certainly no evidence of any saintly assistance with my labours for the rest of the day.

Abdulla, the water thief, who wore a calico skull-cap and a broad grin throughout the proceedings, was a particular problem. Nobody had been able to understand why his strip of land produced twice the normal crop of melons.

'The Will of Allah,' he had always claimed.

His cunning was now exposed. He had constructed an underground channel to feed his crop between the bottom of the public irrigation channel and the bed of the Sheikh Suliman stream.

'Twenty sacks of melons to be forfeited,' I decreed. Abdulla's good teeth glinted in the sun.

'And one for Your Lordship, maybe,' he murmured. I treated this flagrant insinuation of corruption with short shrift.

'I don't like melons,' I said.

The carpet beater found me in a more temperate mood. 'A conditional discharge,' I decreed, before turning to the last case of the morning.

'Guilty with extenuating circumstances,' explained Mr Joshi, the counterfeit artist. His English was as impeccable as his dress. A Bombay silversmith by origin, he had travelled widely and expensively.

The Marie Thérèse dollars which Mr Joshi had fraudulently reproduced in his private mint were still the common currency of South Arabia. Dutch traders of the eighteenth century had first introduced the coins into the country. Holland was then part of the Holy Roman Empire, so the coins bore the curvaceous effigy of the Holy Roman Empress.

The 'extenuating circumstances' proved to be the demands of Mr Joshi's creditors. He had a long record of fraud, including many convictions in India for counterfeiting. I put off sentencing in his case, so that the police inspector could obtain more details of his past.

'Wise sentencing is the mark of a good judge.' This was the oft-repeated mot of the Learned Bencher who had finally sanctioned my call to the Bar.

I'd like to see him getting the scales right under these sort of pressures, I remember thinking.

In some cases, imprisonment was unfortunately the only proper sentence. But sending the defendant to prison was not always the end of the matter, as I discovered on an early visit to the barbers.

'British hair cut?' inquired the proprietor as I stood hesitantly under his sign, 'High Society Saloon', at the corner of the Suk.

'Just a trim,' I decided. The saloon keeper guided me past several chickens into the vacant chair.

'Cheap at any price,' he declared. He was referring to the haircut, not to the chair, from which one spring protruded even more savagely than the other. This set me at a quaint angle, but since the cracked mirror on the wall was similarly inclined, vision, at least, was not inconvenienced.

'What hairstyle are you wanting?' asked my host, handing me some curry-stained photographs of Rudolf Valentino, Lloyd George and ex-King Carol of Rumania.

'Finish,' he interrupted, tired of my indecision, 'I give light crop.' He tucked a piece of gunny bag about me.

'No damn hairs running down the body,' he explained. From under his turban, he produced an elderly pair of scissors and set to work.

'Big job this,' complained the barber after a while. He was snorting horribly, like a boxer. 'Ali,' he yelled. A shrivelled brown acolyte appeared from behind the curtain. 'Bring clippers.' These were kept in a glass case by the door. His mission fulfilled, Ali stood by, twitching admiringly. 'Thinning out,' instructed the craftsman. He now had the slipper-gears hopelessly enmeshed in my hair. 'Needing a bit of oil,' he observed, hurrying outside.

It was a long wait, especially with the clippers suspended from my locks. Ali lit a joss stick to keep back the flies. His master returned at last. 'Bob your uncle,' he proclaimed, emptying a jar of Macassar oil over me. By twisting forward I could glimpse his handiwork in the looking-glass. I had been given a fringe like Henry V at Agincourt. 'Good job,' smirked the hairstylist behind me.

'How's about a nose-cut?' he inquired, pointing to his own hirsute nostrils. I shook my battered head. 'Righty,' he countered, 'I give free massage.' Before I could decline, he was already grinding his knuckles into my scalp.

'You Government fellow?' whispered Ali sympathetically. By this time the Maître had begun to shave my neck with a sharp knife.

'Er, judicial,' I rejoined. My face received an even closer inspection.

'You District Judge!' exclaimed the barber. I nodded. 'My brother knows you,' he mused, scraping away near my jugular. 'You send him to prison last week.' I held firmly to the sides of the chair. The hairdresser took another mouthful of red betel-nut. 'You very hard man,' he announced, baring his crimson teeth.

'I'd prefer not to discuss the case,' I said, levering myself up out of the chair. The helpful Ali began to dust my jacket with a piece of rag, but his employer was not to be deterred.

'My brother,' he declared, 'he got two wifes and seventeen childrens.' He patted his ample stomach. 'And I got the hunger with keeping them.'

Other customers were gathering around with interest.

'I'm sorry about that,' I said, 'but I'm afraid your brother's case was a bad one. He had a great number of previous convictions and not one of those watches he received has been recovered.'

I paid the barber his fee, together with a tip. He was still not satisfied.

'You like to buy hair tonic,' he insisted, indicating several bottles of vivid green elixir at the back of a showcase. 'Oh, very well,' I agreed wearily.

This mollified him. He put his arm into the case and in doing so pulled back his grimy cuff. By a strange coincidence he had a brand new watch on his wrist.

Mere suspicion, as English judges have so frequently explained to juries at home and abroad, has never been enough to justify any conclusion under our law. So there was no aftermath to my visit to that particular barber. And yet the incident was a pointer to some of the other strange happenings I was to encounter overseas. 'It is not,' reported an English Parliamentary Committee, 'from the judges that the most accurate and satisfactory evidence of the effect of the English criminal law can reasonably be expected. They only see the exterior of criminal proceedings after they are brought into a court of justice. Of the cases that never appear there, and of the causes that prevent their appearance they can know nothing. Of the motives which influence the testimony of witnesses, they can form but a hasty and inadequate estimate. Even in the grounds of verdicts, they may often be deceived. From many opportunities of observing the influence of punishment upon those men among whom malefactors are most commonly found, they are by their duties, placed at a great distance.'

Beginning perhaps with my visit to the Arabian hairdresser, my own experience as Judge, especially in my subsequent posting to the Pacific Territories, was not to be quite as the English Parliamentary Committee had suggested. There was less of the 'great distance' than imagined, and sometimes, it seemed, none at all.

9

Levelling the Score

Langford-Smith had exaggerated the situation; my career had not ended in the Middle East.

A search in the vaults of the Old Colonial Office, Sanctuary Buildings, SW1, uncovered the original archive of which my lost file was only a copy. A new file was opened, and the following Christmas saw me in Fulala, an administrative centre in the British South Pacific Territories, replacing, as circuit judge, a chap called Donaldson. I had exchanged the date palms of Arabia for the coconuts of the South Seas.

After disembarking from the ship, my first priority was a courtesy call on the District Commissioner. His was a rambling house overlooking the bay. I had only got as far as the verandah steps when his Alsatian began to remove the seat of my trousers.

'Odd,' said the Commissioner, a tall, balding figure, who was watching with an air of puzzled detachment, 'Judge Donaldson never had the slightest trouble with Rover.'

After a few minutes he called the dog to heel and put down a bowl of water.

'Same for me,' I said, 'with a drop of whisky, maybe.'

'Hope you've brought a few bottles with you,' the Commissioner observed. 'The Fulalans enjoy a bit of the Christmas Spirit. Donaldson's parties were famous at this time of year.'

'In British Arabia,' I said, 'my earlier station, one learned to keep away from alcohol. Mohammedan feeling and all that.'

A shadow seemed to cross the Commissioner's face.

'Well, what about our Boxing Day Bridge Four?' he continued. 'Judge Donaldson's departure has left a real gap there. Of course, he was a champion. Represented Wangunui, New Zealand, five years running.'

I shook my head. 'Scrabble is my game, I'm afraid.'

The Commissioner stood up. It was obviously time to go. I held out my hand and wished him a happy Christmas. To my surprise he dealt me a sharp blow on the forehead with his airmail copy of *The Times*.

'That'll teach you,' he snapped. 'Little beggar!'

'I didn't mean . . .' I began.

'Damned mosquito,' he explained. 'And you'll get a lot more of them at the Judge's Residence. The Malololo Swamp, you know. Donaldson was immune to them,' he added, as he saw me to the door. Outside, the court usher was waiting for me with my trunk on his head.

It was only a brief trot through the mangroves to Donaldson's house, a Tropical Tudor edifice with bamboo gables and a black-painted verandah. Inside it looked as though Donaldson had left in a hurry. An assortment of mildewed caps and topees decorated the hatstand, along with golfing umbrellas, shooting sticks and a climbing crampon. An immense rhino-head glowered down from the end of the dining-room. Propped up on the table, on the back of an old invitation to the Samoa Grand Masters Masonic Banquet, was a note from Donaldson.

'Have left you a few bequests,' it read, 'some sporting togs, a trophy or two, and Hibiscus, the gardener's daughter.'

I was taking a shower when Hibiscus arrived. A biggish lady, she was carrying a loofah, a pumice stone and a long-handled brush.

'Judge Donaldson always liked me to do his back,' she said.

Clothing myself in a tablet of medicated soap, I retreated into the bedroom. 'I'll be in touch,' I called through the door. I was already late for my evening appointment.

My next-door neighbour, Ursula St Alban, had left a message with the Commissioner inviting me to share her Christmas Eve duck. Miss St Alban was the headmistress of the Government School for the Daughters of Chiefs.

'This was a little tradition I always kept up with Rory Donaldson,' she told me as we sat down at the festive table. 'Cynthia Donaldson always flew home to the children for Christmas.' Behind her glasses her eyes gleamed as she leaned forward to light the candles.

'Hope you've got your robes in your baggage,' she went on. 'Rory always wore his judge's scarlet when he gave out the presents around the Fulala Hospital Tree on Christmas afternoon.' She chuckled. 'The nurses gave him a cotton-wool beard to make him into a real Father Christmas. Of course, he had the figure for it.' She gazed wistfully out into the moonlight. 'Great big chappie that he was!'

At that moment the cook reappeared from the kitchen, and before I could speak, Miss St Alban had installed a second helping of Christmas pudding on my plate. 'My Senior Cookery girls are dab hands at this,' she explained. 'Rory Donaldson always asked for more.' I slipped the second helping into my pocket. Fortunately I was able to dispose of it when I popped into the garden to avail myself of the al-fresco facilities. By the time I returned, there were joss sticks burning and Miss St Alban was playing her recording of Grieg's 'Sleigh Ride'. Further conversation was unnecessary until, with a dying fall, the gramophone battery petered out. This gave me a chance to make my farewell.

'Don't forget next Saturday night,' said Miss St Alban, laying a hand on my arm. 'You're partnering me at the New Year Ball. It was an annual date with the Judge.'

The ball was in full swing when we arrived at the Planter's Club. At the bar I found a drink already lined up for me.

'Rum, vodka and pineapple juice, laced with cherry-brandy,' announced the President. 'The Judge's favourite

New Year tipple. Otherwise known as Donaldson's Death Dart.'

'Just a shandy,' I told him, 'and a dry sherry for Miss St Alban.'

'I'll take the Death Dart,' the Headmistress declared. She was somewhat flushed from a vigorous Paul Jones in which I had not succeeded in finding a partner. I hoped this was in no way a reflection upon my appearance.

'Is anything the matter?' Miss St Alban asked, as she whisked me into the President's Waltz. 'You look as if you'd lost a stone since you came to my Christmas Eve Dinner.'

There had, in fact, been some intestinal after-effects on Christmas morning. Indeed, my engagement at the Hospital that afternoon had proved something of a life-saver—thanks to the medical orderly, who provided a quick tot of magnesia from the dispensary.

However the trouble this time was the jacket I was wearing.

'Haven't I seen it somewhere before?' inquired Miss St Alban, peering at the green mould spots which Hibiscus's sponging had failed to remove.

'You probably have,' I said. 'The suitcase with my own dinner jacket hasn't arrived. Hibiscus came up with this old one of Judge Donaldson's.' Too late I realised I should have asked the gardener's daughter to move the buttons. Even so, my safety-pin might have held if I had not tried a double-chasse with Miss St Alban under the plastic mistletoe. I paused to release myself.

'Hibiscus's father wasn't all that keen to let me have it. He wears it for gardening, you see.'

'I can see that all right,' said Miss St Alban.

We sat the next dance out while my partner applied a small spray of eau-de-cologne to her corsage. The next minute a meaty hand dropped on my shoulder.

'Bonzer Burke,' announced an Australian voice in my ear. 'Just a quick word with you, sport.' I stood up to be confronted by a red-faced person with a can of lager in his hand.

'Gonner be meetin' in court next week, Judge. Little problem with the Bank. Can count on yer to see me right, eh, Cobber?'

'I'm afraid not,' I replied stiffly.

No doubt Mr Burke's behaviour was due to an excess of New Year's Eve punch, earlier in the celebrations. Best not to show my true feelings in view of the occasion, I decided.

'The solemn maxim of *sub judice* is imperative,' was all I told him. His response was to crunch a beer-can slowly in his hand and thrust it inside my cummerbund. 'Try getting another beer under your belt, mate,' he joked as he lurched away.

I could see that such flagrant attempts to corrupt new blood on the Bench would have to be dealt with as soon as possible. On the platform Harry Aloha and his Royal Hawaiians were launching into 'White Christmas'. Regrettably I felt in no mood for merrymaking. I had one of my headaches coming on. By now Miss St Alban was well away, in the arms of the District Commissioner. I pondered whether to break in to make my apologies, but decided perhaps another time would do. I stepped outside, only to be confronted by another dilemma. The Island Taxi was nowhere to be seen.

Fortunately one of the club servants stepped into the breach. He offered me the loan of his bicycle for the journey home along the coast-road. The trade-wind had got up and blown a few coconuts on the road. Otherwise I don't think I would have fallen off. Certainly not in front of the police station.

A burly figure appeared in the doorway.

'Bit too much at the club, sir?' called the constable, a giant Fulalan. 'New Year Party eh, man?'

He laughed reprovingly and brought out a large notebook. 'What to say? Drunk driving? Obstruct highway?'

'Look here, officer,' I said, 'this was an accident.'

I was struggling to straighten the handlebars, gripping the front wheel between my knees. The constable walked round to the other side.

'No rear light,' he announced. He grinned down at me. 'OK. Christmas is Christmas. Make just a warning, this time.' Clearly he had no idea of my identity.

An extraordinary thought flashed through my mind. Here was a startling chance to show Mr Bonzer Burke, and his like, precisely where I stood in the great matter of Judicial Impartiality!

I stood up and faced the constable. 'Prosecute me,' I said.

A look of astonishment passed over the constable's face when I gave him my name and address. Yet this was nothing to the expression of total disbelief registered by the Court Registrar as I tried to explain the situation next morning.

'The principle is good, sir, I agree,' he stammered, 'but who will conduct the proceedings? There's no other judge within a thousand miles.'

'Then I shall try myself,' I decreed.

It was developing into a tricky situation. Nevertheless, there was no going back now. With much shaking of the head the Registrar eventually agreed to list the case for a special holiday hearing.

I must admit to some feelings of tension on the following Friday. I would be one of the few HM Judges to experience the harsh reality of what it would be like to be on the wrong side of the law. I discarded my old university tie for a sober black one, and held my head high as I walked into my little thatched court-house.

A camera clicked as I mounted the steps.

'*Pacific Islands Gazette*,' called a muffled voice from behind a photographer's hood. 'Big smile, Judge.' I blushed. This, I told myself, was something I had to go through with—although it was a pretty embarrassing start to the year.

Inside, the courthouse was full to its doors. All heads

craned as I took my place at the wicker rail. The Registrar read out the charge.

'Guilty or not guilty?' he mumbled.

'Speak up,' I called. He repeated the question.

'Guilty,' I answered. There was an excited buzz from the audience.

I stepped down and took my familiar place on the Bench.

'This type of offence,' I said, addressing the now empty dock, 'is not to be overlooked.'

I paused to consider a suitable penalty. It would be counter-productive, I decided, to cross-examine myself for details of mitigation. The slightest hint of the ridiculous would ruin the whole purpose of the exercise.

Without more ado, I imposed a sharp fine of £10. There was a round of applause from the onlookers as I left the Bench.

'What are you smiling about?' I asked the Registrar in chambers afterwards.

'I think about Judge Donaldson,' he replied. My heart sank.

'Judge Donaldson. Never would do that thing,' he added. 'Too proud man.' He laid on the table a jingling package tied up with a discarded piece of Christmas tinsel. 'Whip-round from the court staff. Towards the fine!' I was deeply touched.

'Congratulations, sir,' he said. 'Best man wins.'

Perhaps my New Year resolution had laid the shadow of Donaldson, at least for the time being.

10

Trial by Jury in the South Seas

Historically, the earliest of my predecessors as a British
Judge in the South Seas was the famous Knight of the
Sandwich Isles, Charles St Stephen. His legal career had
started in Sydney, where he was the Law Reporter. A
wanderer by temperament, St Stephen was soon travelling
in Oceania. Succumbing to the spell of Robert Louis
Stevenson's Golden Isles, he became Hawaiian Chargé
d'Affaires for Southern Polynesia. In reward for his
services in this exotic post, he was knighted by the
Sovereign of the Sandwich Isles.

His last post in the South Pacific was in Fulala. There he
became the British Resident Judge under Tombi, the
Cannibal King of Bua.

The first case heard by Sir Charles, in his midget court-
house on the hillside of King Tombi's capital, Fulala,
reflected the bizarre disorder of that beachcombing community. It concerned a Filipino known as Looey, the cook
on a labour schooner, who had killed a fellow sailor with a
knife. Sir Charles condemned him to death. Looey was to
be hanged on the morning of 27th May, 1872. All
preparations for the execution had been completed, but the
hangman had failed to appear because of his wife's illness.
The execution had therefore been postponed. Looey's
lawyer at once petitioned the Chief Justice to secure the
condemned man's release on the ground that the sentence
had not been carried out as directed. Sir Charles dismissed
the application. He ordered the hanging to take place next
morning. At 7 a.m. on 29th May, Looey was again placed
over the trap. However, the rope, left in position overnight,

had become swollen by the rain and would not run in the noose. When the hangman pulled the bolt, the noose caught upon Looey's chin. Stunned by the drop, Looey hung for about ten minutes. Then he began to struggle, calling to the bystanders to shoot him and end his misery. The only solution was to cut the rope. Looey was returned to his cell while King Tombi and Sir Charles were consulted. The King granted a reprieve, but for Sir Charles, the 'Looey case' was not over. In preparation for his execution, Looey had made a will directing how his savings were to be distributed. He returned from the scaffold to find his directions already carried out. His money had been spent upon a merry rum-party by his grief-stricken friends. Sir Charles resolved the problem by arranging compensation for Looey out of public funds. Looey remained in the Fulala jail for some years and was then deported.

During 1873, various up-country tribes rebelled against King Tombi. Learning that several hundred insurrectionists had been captured, Sir Charles advised the King to indict them for high treason. I was able to study the case records of Sir Charles, still preserved in the Circuit Archives. His notes of evidence were pencilled in a shaky hand. Court sittings were short, with frequent adjournments to one or other of the fifty-two public houses in the settlement. Applying the principle that everyone who appeared before him was either guilty or a fool, Sir Charles convicted everybody. He awarded long terms of imprisonment in all cases, but the prisoners served their sentences in an unusual way. They were hired out by the King to work for European planters in Vola Seru, the main island of the group.

At times, Sir Charles sat with an assistant judge, an island noble unversed in the law, who had great difficulty in understanding the English language. For this problem the Lord Chief Justice had an immediate solution. The only way to make a foreigner understand English was to shout at him. Thus, instead of discreetly whispering the instructive passage in his volume of English Criminal Law to his brother judge on the bench, Sir Charles would bellow the whole chapter into the poor man's ear—much to the irritation of anglers in the river nearby.

Sir Charles favoured jury trial in the Islands. In Fulala he obtained the assistance of European jurors, some of whom were peculiarly well versed in court procedure. These were the escaped convicts from Australia, who had acquired their knowledge in the dock at the Old Bailey.

Outside the capital, jurymen were less easily recruited. Sir Charles used to tell a story of a visit he made to an outlying island in the Bua Group.

The Judge had reached a remote village in the middle of the island. There he planned to hold court. The village chief had one prisoner awaiting trial—upon a charge of murder.

'We must first empanel a jury,' directed Sir Charles from his barkcloth litter under the coconut trees. His interpreter explained to the villagers what was required. 'Swear in the twelve good men and true,' the judge proceeded. After hearing the evidence, Sir Charles summed up to the jury. 'Consider your verdict, gentlemen,' he concluded. The jurors retired to a nearby thicket.

Sir Charles was preparing for a paddle in the lagoon when his interpreter rushed up to him.

'Come quickly, lordship,' he urged, 'there is great trouble.' Easing on his mosquito boots, Sir Charles answered the call of duty.

It seemed that fighting had broken out among the jurors. By the time he had reached the fracas, four of the jurymen were unconscious, the rest stood around in hang-dog silence. All bore marks of violence.

'Am I to assume, gentlemen,' Sir Charles inquired, 'that you are not agreed upon your verdict?' There was no reply.

'Bear in mind,' he went on, 'the jury must fast until a verdict is reached. Neither fire, food nor candle, as the English Common Law has it.'

Sir Charles withdrew to his *lakalunoa*, the palm-leaf canopy customarily erected by the Buans for visitors of importance. The long, sticky afternoon drew to a close. At dusk the air became cooler and Sir Charles, exhausted by his long journey, fell asleep. When he opened his eyes again it was already sunrise.

'We shall resume court at once,' he told the interpreter. He returned to the coconut grove—'Mother Nature's Old Bailey', as he referred to it.

'Where's the prisoner?' he demanded, the jury having appeared.

'It was a long, hungry night for them, lordship,' stammered the interpreter, indicating the jurors as they filed into their bamboo box. 'Cannibal customs die hard in these islands.'

'Poor wretch,' Sir Charles would conclude, when recounting the tale to his paling dinner guests, 'he was simply the victim of a unanimous verdict.'

Fortunately, well before my own arrival in the South Pacific, juries were fed at Government expense.

11

The Shark God's Revenge

'Gentlemen of the Jury,' I began, from under the shade of a palm tree, 'kindly gather round for the summing up.'

My new duties had begun in earnest, and I was on circuit in Bua, the very part of the South Pacific known to Sir Charles St Stephen. Like him, I was holding court in a village clearing.

'Under the English legal system,' I told the seven impassive Buan jurors, 'we each have our separate role. You, the Jury, decide the facts. I, the Judge, decide the law.'

It seemed a simple enough case in which the evidence of guilt was overwhelming. The defendant, a fisherman by trade, was charged with stealing a canoe. The prosecution had been conducted by the Island Inspector, who suddenly interrupted the proceedings at that point.

'The defendant is wanting to give evidence,' he explained.

'But he's already refused to do that,' I said. 'Section 219 of the Criminal Procedure (Pacific Islands) Ordinance is clear on the question of re-opened testimony.'

The Inspector cleared his throat.

'This is a very special case, sir,' he emphasised.

I was unmoved.

'But the canoe was taken within the waters of our sacred Shark God,' he went on.

'What's that got to do with it?' I said.

He rolled his eyes.

I had momentarily forgotten the provisions of the Overseas Territories Order in Council of 1894. These stipulated that 'account be taken in all cases of local usage and custom.'

'So where do we go from here?' I asked.

The Inspector pointed upwards to the looming cliff on the side of the lagoon.

'Defendant has to take an oath of his innocence in the Shark God's Temple,' he said.

Through the mist I could just detect the opening of a cave. The monsoon had begun and a downpour seemed imminent.

'Hadn't we better adjourn until the weather changes?' I said.

'Justice delayed is justice denied,' the Inspector reminded me.

He had attended a course for Commonwealth Constabularies at Eastbourne, and had already displayed, during the course of the trial, an irritating fondness for such phrases.

I made a quick estimate of the size of the climbing party—seven jurors, the Inspector, defendant and self.

On leave in the early 'fifties, a friend had persuaded me to join a Beginners' Climbing Club in Snowdonia, an interesting venture until a loose crampon had put me out of action. The experience had made me cautious.

'We'll need to be roped together.'

The Hawaiian Creeper growing all around caught my eye.

The Inspector's face cleared as I demonstrated the knotting together of the twisted lengths of vine.

We followed the Inspector in single file round the headland to the foot of the cliff.

The defendant, a burly giant of a man, gave me a helping hand over some rather slippery seaweed and we soon caught up with the nimble-footed jurors. The Inspector festooned us loosely with the vines.

'Any volunteers for Anchor Man?' I inquired.

There were some problems of interpretation but the defendant was finally drafted into this position.

We had got up a good thirty feet when the rains began.

The steps disappeared as water poured down the gullies, muddying the track.

'I'm not Sherpa Tensing,' I told the Inspector. 'The expedition will have to be adjourned *sine die*.'

But once again the Inspector was on the ball.

'Not advisable in a criminal trial, Your Honour,' he said. 'Justice should be swift if it is to be sure.'

Our uphill journey was resumed.

'Follow quick, sir,' the Inspector called. He, and the rest of the party had disappeared into a black hole in the mountainside.

'Couldn't we have some light on things?' I called.

The Inspector was already igniting a crude torch of pandanus leaves. In the flickering light I could see what looked like a primitive altar of stones, adorned with cowrie shells, at the far end of the cave. He indicated that I should be seated, and I took my place on a small boulder in somewhat cramped conditions, between a stalagmite and a stalactite. The jury had settled themselves in a neat cross-legged row against the opposite wall. All eyes were on the defendant. He placed an offering of kava root before the shrine. Next he removed his shirt and anointed his massive frame with a bottle of coconut oil.

'Perhaps we could get a move on with the matter in hand,' I said. 'I do have a fairly heavy list to get through this afternoon.'

The defendant stood to attention, his head bowed in his chest, and spoke in a hoarse voice.

'He says he did not steal the canoe,' the Inspector translated. 'It was washed up to his house by the sea tide.'

Solemnly he placed the defendant's hand on the offering of kava.

'Do you swear before the Shark God, the jury—and of course His Honour—that you are innocent?'

'I swear.'

The solemn silence was broken by a clatter from the altar. One of the pebbles dislodged itself and a large crab emerged. It began to sample the kava. A whisper went up from the jurors.

'Could the Foreman speak up, please,' I interjected.

'The crab is the Spirit of the God,' the Inspector explained. He mopped his forehead with a banana leaf. 'He is eating the words of the defendant. The defendant speaks falsely.'

It seemed time to pull the situation together.

'Gentlemen of the Jury,' I addressed the quivering row. 'Please act coolly on the evidence. I must ask you to recall the basic principles of English law. Is it your verdict that the prisoner is guilty or not guilty?'

'Guilty,' declared the Jury.

The defendant's face was impassive as I finally closed the proceedings.

It was time to make the descent.

The mist had closed in again. This time, secure roping-together would be vital. I supervised the Inspector's efforts closely as he dealt out the length of vine between the three of us. The defendant led the way as before. The jurors had elected to make their own way down.

There was a pause as we were about to start off again.

'Defendant wants to know what sentence Your Lordship has in mind,' said the Inspector from his position between the prisoner and myself.

'I'm afraid the court has other matters on its mind at present,' I said, tightening the vines around my court-jacket.

'He wants you to show mercy, lordship,' the Inspector persisted. 'Give him a chance.'

I was making calculations about my own chance. The standard Alpine Club rope would stop a twelve stone man. What would half a dozen strands of Hawaiian Creeper take with ten?

As we moved downwards, the edge of the cliff seemed unusually close.

'Defendant says he would abandon his life of crime,' said the Inspector. 'Pull himself up.'

That was more than I could do at that moment. A treacherous stone had slipped as I was rounding the bend to the track below. Fortunately the creeper was holding.

'I'm giving it very serious consideration,' I announced with what confidence I could muster. I grabbed for a hand-hold on the rock face. The defendant was watching impassively from the safety of a spur below. His hand moved on the rope. Between us, the Inspector looked up pleadingly.

As it happened, the final decision was made for me. Worn through by the edge of the rock, the creeper gave way.

'Six months' probation,' I called as I swung past.

The next second I was grasped in the arms of the contrite defendant.

'Okay, Judge?' asked the Inspector behind me. I nodded.

'Defendant to lead the way down,' the Inspector called.

'Yes, and tell him to keep to the straight and narrow,' I quipped.

A judicial sense of humour can survive most things. Even the revenge of the Shark God of Bua.

However, my reaction to odd situations was soon to be put to a fresh test.

A directive was waiting for me in Fulala when I returned. It came from my boss, Sir Neville Gawsby. Sir Neville was the Chief Justice for all the British territories in that part of the world.

'I want you to take evidence on commission for me,' he wrote from his office in the antipodean capital, 'I am conducting an Official Government Inquiry into South Pacific Fishing Rights. The evidence I should like you to obtain is from a European lady called Miss Wotherspoon. She has lived her whole life on an island 230 miles west of Bua. The lady is said to have invaluable local knowledge relevant to my Inquiry. She refuses to travel, so you will have to try to record her testimony *in situ*.'

I made the necessary arrangements and set sail without delay.

12

Miss Wotherspoon's Island

Miss Wotherspoon's island is easily missed. Tasman never found it, Bligh avoided it, Cook, blown off course by a hurricane, nearly ran into it. I managed to land there safely in a local copra boat.

'Where shall I find her?' I asked the skipper.

'She lives on the plantation,' he answered. He pointed to a patch of green beyond the beach. 'Think you're wasting your time, though,' he added. 'Sounds rather like a lot of red tape, this Government Inquiry.' He had agreed to pick me up later, on the evening tide.

'The Chief Justice would not send me all this way for nothing,' I assured him.

He shook his head.

'It's a weird place in any case,' he said. 'And as for Miss Wotherspoon . . . !'

With the sun glinting on the pink coral, against a dazzling backcloth of hibiscus and oleander, the island looked enchanting.

'Wait until it gets dark,' warned the captain. 'None of the workers on her plantation will go out except in daylight.'

I made some wry comment about superstitions of Polynesia. He shook his head.

'It's an island of ghosts,' he insisted.

I threw my briefcase on to the jetty and sprang ashore.

'Well, Miss Wotherspoon doesn't seem to mind them,' I laughed.

She had inherited the island a few years ago from her father, Algernon Wotherspoon. Mr Wotherspoon was a descendant of early English settlers from the mainland.

'It's different for her,' called the copra-master, returning to the wheel, 'she's . . .' The rest of his words were lost in the wind as he swung his craft out to sea.

A few minutes' brisk walking through the coconut groves brought me to a clearing. A tropical garden to the left of the main drive seemed to be ornamented with large boulders.

'A pygmy Stonehenge?' I wondered. I had always been a keen amateur archaeologist. I pulled aside the creepers on the nearest stone. There seemed to be traces of ancient hieroglyphics carved into the surface.

With some excitement I put on my spectacles and read, 'Called to Higher Service, Reginald Wotherspoon, June 29th 1903'. I had merely stumbled on the family cemetery.

There were no less than a dozen similar monuments, and the last of these was freshly decorated in the traditional native style with streamers of coloured grass. From here I looked up and saw the house ahead of me. It was a great rambling bungalow crammed with the flotsam of 100 years of squirearchical living, South Pacific style.

'Anybody at home?' I called, taking a few more steps. The main room was full of Victorian chairs and tables squeezed up next to a huge Hawaiian day-bed. Landseer prints on the walls rubbed shoulders with native axes and ceremonial whales' teeth.

'Blue, tending to mauve,' said a voice from the shadows.

'Ah!' I jumped.

A very pale lady in a barkcloth shawl was examining me from a wicker chair on the opposite side of the parlour.

'Miss Wotherspoon, I presume.'

She put down her lorgnette.

'I'm the Circuit Judge,' I said, introducing myself. I showed her the papers from the Chief Justice. 'As you see, Sir Neville wants me to take what we lawyers call evidence on commission. Will it be convenient for you to answer certain questions?'

'More mauve than blue,' repeated Miss Wotherspoon.

'Sorry?'

'Your astral body,' she said.

With the aid of a walking-stick, she pulled up a cane table and rang a bell.

'At least you're in time for tea,' she continued.

I sat on the edge of a sofa.

'As the documents make clear, ma'am,' I plunged on, 'the Chief Justice is inquiring into the appropriate royalties payable for crayfish trawled in this area of Oceania. Sir Neville has been told you are well acquainted with customary fishing practice in the islands. He feels your knowledge will be especially useful in his Inquiry.'

Miss Wotherspoon continued to gaze through me, as it were.

'Distinctly mauve,' she muttered.

I glanced over my shoulder. Apart from a little dandruff on my collar, I could detect nothing.

'I thought the astral body only appeared after one was dead, Miss Wotherspoon,' I japed.

'It all depends,' she replied quietly. 'Sugar or lemon?'

A native girl had glided silently in with a silver tray of Dresden china and, equally silently, out again.

'Lemon,' I said.

My hostess poured a delicate cupful of tea from a fluted urn and handed me a silver dish of sliced lemon and a guava sandwich.

'On second thoughts, I think I'll take sugar,' I said.

'A vacillator,' reproved Miss Wotherspoon. 'Mauve always goes with vacillating characters. My late father was quite the opposite. His astral body is bright red, of course.'

'Is he still around, then?' I asked. It seemed as well to humour the old girl.

'He most certainly is,' was the reply.

'I noticed some decorations on the last grave,' I said. She nodded.

'It's the anniversary of father's death tomorrow.'

I swallowed the rest of my sandwich rather too quickly and turned again to the contents of my briefcase.

'All I have to do, Miss Wotherspoon,' I said, 'is to record your answers to these questions. It won't take long.' I opened my Court Notebook.

'There's a comfortable bed for you in the guest suite,' she interjected, 'but you may be a little troubled by the bats.' She pointed to a vast ivi tree which overshadowed the East wing of the house. Dusk was falling and from its branches I could hear the shrieks of its webbed inhabitants.

'It won't be necessary for me to stay overnight,' I said, 'but it's kind of you to offer.'

The noiseless servant girl removed the tea things and lit the kerosene lights.

'Thank you, Tupou,' said her mistress. The whites of Tupou's eyes rolled in my direction as she withdrew. The only sound, apart from the bats, was the hissing of the lamps.

'It must be very lonely for you out here,' I remarked.

Miss Wotherspoon pointed through the shutters to the long deserted sweep of grey sand curving into the distance.

'Dreadfully overcrowded,' she replied.

I ventured a discreet laugh.

'With spirits,' said Miss Wotherspoon.

I unscrewed my fountain-pen firmly.

'If you would just answer questions one to ten for a start,' I began.

'All the Departed Souls of Polynesia gather here,' continued Miss Wotherspoon, 'on their way to Nirvana.'

'A sort of refuelling station,' I murmured. The joke fell flat.

'It's the last shore they touch before the long sea journey to the Great Beyond in the far West. But for some reason father doesn't seem to want to take the plunge with the rest of them.'

I tried a no-nonsense approach.

'Perhaps we needn't go through the questionnaire in

detail,' I said briskly. 'All the Chief Justice needs to know is what fish have been traditionally caught in this and neighbouring islands and in what manner. Now I understand that as a child you used to go out with the local fishermen?'

Miss Wotherspoon cocked her head to one side.

'It's him,' she said. The shutters were rattling a little—no doubt the breeze was blowing in from the sea.

'Was it customary, Miss Wotherspoon,' I persisted, 'for the islanders to take crayfish?'

'It's father,' said Miss Wotherspoon. 'He always seems to be especially out of sorts round about his anniversary. I wish I knew why.'

I removed my spectacles with a sigh of exasperation. 'A point of relevance in the Chief Justice's Inquiry, Miss Wotherspoon,' I explained patiently, 'is that if the islanders merely fish for tuna, then the royalties payable for crayfish will be very modest. This is where you can help.'

There was a curious pattering sound on the corrugated iron roof overhead.

'He really is irritable tonight,' said Miss Wotherspoon. 'He wouldn't be on the roof unless he was wound up about something.'

I began to pack up my papers.

'Sir Neville did hope you could help in this inquiry, ma'am,' I expostulated, 'but of course there's no legal obligation on your part.' While I was speaking the door opened and a bowl of dried leaves rustled in the breeze.

'Can't you possibly try and tell me what's the matter?' demanded Miss Wotherspoon.

'It's just simply that I don't seem to be getting any co-operation from you in this matter,' I replied stiffly, 'so I might as well be on my way.'

'Why didn't you tell me before?' exclaimed Miss Wotherspoon.

'I thought you appreciated the purpose of my visit,' I answered.

'I'm not speaking to you, Judge,' she said, her gaze fixed

upon her empty hand. 'My father has this moment come in and handed me this astral note. It reads,' she continued in unflurried tones, '"Buried wrong way round. Kindly reverse as soon as possible".'

'So they go in for telegrams in the after-life?' I chided.

'You should be the last person to jest about this, Judge,' rejoined Miss Wotherspoon, 'when it's your presence here that has enabled him to achieve this final breakthrough.'

'Mine?' I demurred.

'You're the first white man to visit us since father's death, and you've no doubt provided that special missing link in the psychic chain.'

She took me by the hand.

'Mauve astrals often have the power.'

She inspected me with some concern.

'I notice you've turned a bit paler blue. Do you feel tired?' she inquired. 'Loss of ectoplasm is quite a debilitating experience.'

'I do feel a bit on the groggy side,' I said. 'So if you'll forgive me I'll get back to my bunk on board.' I was thinking of the medicinal brandy I had tucked away there.

'You could help with the spade-work tomorrow morning,' suggested Miss Wotherspoon.

I had tried my hand in various strange ways during my time on the Overseas Bench, but this was a case for drawing the line.

'Better left to the undertaker,' I said.

'All we have in the way of an undertaker on this island,' Miss Wotherspoon rejoined, 'is Tupou's uncle. And he put father back to front in the first place, poor man.'

'Well I'm sure he'll get it right tomorrow morning,' I soothed, 'and that should see your father safely off the premises.'

'Let's hope so,' rejoined Miss Wotherspoon. 'Call again next year and see.'

She rang the bell. 'Here's Tupou with the lamp to see you down the drive.'

The girl with the rolling eyes was at my elbow as I made my farewell.

The moment came for Tupou and me to pass the decorated grave. The coloured garlands shone in the light.

'Everybody make present for Mr Wotherspoon,' explained Tupou, holding the lamp over the grave. 'Now you must put something.'

'I don't happen to have a wreath with me,' I snorted.

'Any little thing,' she hissed, 'or you get Bad Luck.' She looked pointedly at my briefcase.

'There's nothing in here,' I said, irritably snapping it open. Her eye fell on the pink ribbon around the Inquiry Papers.

'Look nice,' she commanded.

The next moment, several feet of Government red tape were being plaited by Tupou into a makeshift garland.

Tupou left me at the compound gate. As I wended my way through a dark thicket of fern, I looked back and caught a last glimpse of my offering hanging lop-sided in the place of honour on top of the stone.

With a hoarse cry a large bird flapped unexpectedly across my path.

'Lucky I'm not superstitious,' I told myself.

Once on the empty shore I had a distinct feeling of something or someone behind. Perhaps it was a family of crabs scuttling for shelter when I passed. 'Extraordinary how credulous some people get,' I thought.

I arrived at the jetty to the welcoming beacon of the copra boat.

'How did you get on?' asked the skipper as I stepped aboard.

I looked back to the lights of Miss Wotherspoon's bungalow twinkling in the distance.

'You were quite right,' I said. 'It was just a matter of Government red tape after all.'

My report to Chief Justice Sir Neville Gawsby must have disappointed him, but he made no comment.

'Proceed by Fiji Airways into Western Micronesia,' he minuted, 'you should find the normal circuit work there pretty straightforward.'

That was not quite how it turned out.

13

A Session at Sabu-Sabu

To begin with, I was unlucky with the weather.

I had just settled into my room at the Airport Hotel, Fandi, when the monsoon broke. The first thunderbolt struck the tin roof directly over my head.

'Are you all right?' called the manager, above the downpour.

'Yes,' I replied. 'The telephone is dead, not me.'

I had been speaking to Winston Moko, the Court Registrar at Sabu-Sabu, the principal township on the other side of the island. I was due to hold the main session there next day.

'Is official transport provided?' I asked him. At that vital point the storm cut us off. It seemed that I would have to fend for myself.

By 10 a.m. the following morning I was on my way. I had hired the island's only self-drive motorcar, a pre-war model inscribed 'Boomerang Service. There and Back in No Time'. The coastal road was littered with the debris of the storm. I needed every ounce of driving skill to avoid the fallen coconuts and banana-fronds, but the trickiest part of the journey was the estuary. Done it, I congratulated myself after negotiating the ford successfully. I spoke too soon. I had proceeded only a short distance along the track on the other side when, with a tell-tale splutter, the vehicle seized up. After a long wait by the roadside I was thankful to see a lorry coming up behind me. It was carrying a sort of bamboo cage on the back. The tiny cab in front was only just big enough for the driver, a grim looking official in a dark-blue uniform.

'I simply must get to Sabu-Sabu,' I explained, after waving him to a halt.

He jerked a thumb at the rising waters of the estuary. 'No more traffic this morning,' he replied. 'Too much rain.' I glanced enquiringly at the rear accommodation of his own vehicle. 'You'll not like riding in there,' he said.

'What have you got,' I joked, 'a travelling zoo?'

'A travelling prisoner,' he answered sternly. 'I have to take him to court at Sabu-Sabu for trial.'

A ridiculous quandary. If I let the lorry go on without me there would be no trial.

With considerable misgiving I finally decided to conceal my identity and risk a ride in the cage. Squeezing inside was not so easy either, because of the size of my companion, a tattooed Fijian in an American singlet embroidered 'Peace and Love'.

'Nice of you to give me a lift,' I began but the poor fellow made it clear—by a somewhat embarrassing gesture—that he was in no mood for pleasantries.

We bumped along to our destination in silent discomfort.

Just as we were turning into the court-house compound we ran over a pig. Our driver entered into a passionate argument with the owner of the pig and completely forgot about me.

I shook and hammered the padlocked door of the cage, only to cover myself with oily rust and sand. Eventually a constable put his head out of the court-house.

'If you don't keep quiet in there,' he shouted, 'I'll bring the Judge to you.'

'That won't be necessary,' I called back, 'he's already here.'

The police-officer may have recognised a hint of authority in my voice, because he produced a key and released me.

'Please fetch the Court Registrar,' I directed.

The dapper figure of Winston Moko emerged from the court-house. An islander of Chinese extraction, he was not easily ruffled.

'Welcome to Sabu-Sabu,' he said, with a small bow. 'I see Your Honour obtained official transport after all.'

The case of the tattooed Fijian was quickly solved. I bound him over under the Prevention of Crime Ordinance for threatening his mother-in-law. He left the dock, wearing, according to a subsequent complaint, the Warder's new boots. The rest of the first week in the Session passed uneventfully. The only hitch occurred late on, when the Judge's shower broke down. This occupied a kind of thatched lean-to attached to the court-house—very convenient for a quick cool-off at midday.

'I fix him,' reported Registrar Winston Moko. He was referring to the jammed ballcock in the water-tank. Plumbing was not altogether his line; even so, his makeshift repair—with a strip of barkcloth and a splint of bamboo— might have held if I had been more patient. Twisting across to wrestle with the problem I lost my only pair of spectacles down the drain.

'Still one case left,' Winston reminded me from the other side of the door.

I had given up the idea of a shower and was struggling back into my gown when the limitations of the Registrar's handiwork released a spray of water down my neck.

'Jury getting fed up, sir,' warned the Registrar, giving the door-handle another rattle.

I returned in haste to the Bench, wondering how I was going to manage without my glasses. Fortunately the defendant pleaded guilty to the first count in the indictment —possessing a coconut for use as an offensive weapon— contrary to the Amended Penal Code, and the prosecution elected not to proceed on the other counts. No paperwork was, therefore, involved. I discharged the jury and placed the defendant on probation, with an order for confiscation of the exhibit.

During the adjournment I explained my predicament to Winston Moko. He was busy dividing up our luncheon pineapple.

'Why not visit Mr Bhoybhoy, the island optician?' he advised.

Mr Sunderjee Bhoybhoy, known to friends as Sunny, like many Indian migrants in the South Pacific, had a remarkable talent for commerce. I made my way, that afternoon, to Sabu-Sabu marketplace, and followed a giant hand pointing the way to the 'Bhoybhoy Lucky Emporium. Everything Within'. This was a twin-roofed structure with plaster minarets and the flags of all nations strung in between. I was admiring the display—consisting of photographs of spectacled ladies—when I was joined by the tubby figure of the Proprietor.

'My aunties, my sisters, my cousins,' he explained. 'All are wearing my glasses, every man jack.'

'Surely not that one?' I asked, indicating a portrait of the Queen of Tonga, wearing a pair of suspiciously inked-in frames.

'Advertisement only!' said Mr Bhoybhoy.

He bustled me inside. Every corner was occupied by a different branch of the Bhoybhoy Trading Empire. At the main counter a very small boy was trying, without success, to stack up a load of yams twice his size.

'Number ten son,' explained the patriarch, swiping at the infant with a fly-swat as he passed. 'No-good, lazy fellow.' From the rear of the shop came the spicy smell of Mrs Bhoybhoy's curry. The cook herself beamed out at me over the pile of chappattis that were the chief attraction of the establishment. Behind her I was surprised to see several travel posters advertising 'Cook's Tours of the Orient', and 'British Railways Cheap-Day Excursions'.

'Branch Agency only,' explained Mr Bhoybhoy. He pointed to the postscript: 'Onward Connections Arranged by Bhoybhoy Canoe'.

We climbed a spiral staircase with one or two missing steps. At the top was a red plush curtain emblazoned in the centre with a single glaring eye. Mr Bhoybhoy drew it aside with a flourish.

'Consulting room,' he announced. 'Shall be with you in one minute sharp.'

I took my seat on a two-and-a-half-legged stool. A large spotlight with an orange bulb was trained on Mr Bhoybhoy's framed diploma in ophthalmics from Bombay. Propped against a model of the Taj Mahal was some kind of a test card. To my dismay I could not make out a single letter.

'My eyesight seems to be worse than usual,' I told Mr Bhoybhoy on his return.

'Since when are you reading Urdu?' he asked. He patted my shoulder and produced a card with the usual English letters. I noticed he had slipped on a white coat and a surgical mask. His eyes twinkled above it as he began to tap the back of my head with a small wooden mallet. I was having difficulty in reading the second line, when Mr Bhoybhoy pinned a steel spectacle-frame on to my nose.

'Is very important in your job you are having tip-top sight,' he observed, slipping a succession of different lenses into the frame. He moved back a few paces. 'Say I am in witness box for case of murder.' Mr Bhoybhoy's brows knitted in a scowl. 'You see I am guilty man?' Before I had time to reply, he sprang forward, slipped another lens into position, then returned to his post in the imaginary witness box. 'Now I am under false charge,' he continued. 'You see face of innocent man?'

'It might be easier if you removed your mask,' I pointed out.

But Mr Bhoybhoy had tired of further examination. He brought out a cardboard box marked 'OXO FOR BEEFIER TASTE'.

'You choose,' decreed the optician.

Inside was an assortment of spectacle frames. Every pair seemed to be liberally decorated with sequins.

'Surely these are for ladies?' I said.

'Correct,' agreed Mr Bhoybhoy. 'In Sabu-Sabu is what the womenfolk always want.'

'But haven't you any for men?' I persisted.

'Out of stock,' he replied. 'Next shipment end of month.'

For the time being it seemed I would be obliged to make do with what there was.

'Do you have a hand-mirror on the premises?' I enquired. He did. I held up the looking-glass while positioning the spectacles at various angles. My experiments were interrupted by a sudden flash which I took to be a faulty light-bulb.

'Until August 1st, then,' were my parting words to Mr Bhoybhoy.

Back on the bench with my temporary purchase, it was now possible to take a clear view of the evidence. Naturally my appearance was greeted with a few whistles from the rear of the court, but Winston Moko quickly restored order and, after a few days, interest seemed to die away. Occasionally I tried to manage without the glasses altogether. For routine work—unlicensed pearl-diving, breaches of the liquor laws, illegal belly dancing contrary to the Sabbath Day Ordinance—this presented no difficulty. A deferred sentence, on the other hand, did give rise to confusion. Captain Tojo, skipper of the Japanese whaler, *Madame Butterfly*, had successfully prosecuted his chief engineer for assaulting him on the wharf.

'Violence cannot be tolerated,' I announced, imposing a stiff fine.

'But I am the victim,' came the protest.

The two Orientals, prosecutor and defendant, looked remarkably similar. I soon donned the spectacles to correct my mistake.

'Today is August 1st,' the Registrar reminded me the following week. 'You have appointment with Mr Bhoybhoy.'

'I'll call in on the way from viewing the public works manhole cover,' I told him.

I was hearing an application under the First Schedule to the Dangerous Highways Ordinance. As usual I seemed to have got things the wrong way round.

'Maybe we should have collected your lordship's new

glasses first,' murmured the Registrar, helping me out of the manhole.

It was a tumble I quickly forgot, because a really nasty surprise was waiting for me at the Bhoybhoy Emporium. A small crowd milled about the window. Winston Moko seemed anxious to prevent my joining them.

'What's he got on show today?' I demanded. 'Nothing indecent, I trust?'

'Not quite, my lord,' Winston replied.

I pushed him aside.

There in the centre, instead of the Queen, stood an enlarged photograph of myself, complete with the sequinned spectacles. With dismay I recalled the surreptitious flash in Mr Bhoybhoy's consulting room. The caption underneath was in bold capitals: 'HONORABLE JUDGE LOOK GOOD IN BHOYBHOY SPECTACLES'.

'Look even better in these,' confided a familiar voice at my side.

Mr Bhoybhoy held out a new pair of glasses, with regulation black rims. Trying to control myself, I pointed to the window.

'You should know, Mr Bhoybhoy,' I said evenly, 'using a photograph for commercial purposes without consent is an infringement of the Fairground Provisions. It is a grave statutory breach, involving compensation—if not actual removal of the trading licence.'

Mr Bhoybhoy merely winked.

When the bill arrived at court, I was pleased to note he had made a small deduction for 'services rendered'. My photograph was also returned. It now occupies a rather special place of honour in my album of South Sea souvenirs.

The same album contains another interesting memento, acquired shortly afterwards. This is an autographed portrait of Aubrey St John Pennington, Esquire. He is wearing the uniform of a Colonial Administrative Officer, Grade Two. Which is not how I saw him on the first occasion.

14

A Break in the Circuit

Pennington was the Divisional Commissioner on the Vatuan Archipelago, another group of islands on my circuit. A tall disjointed figure with a wild thatch of hair, in a tattered golfing blazer over army trousers, he was waiting for me at the wharf of the South Island, where I was due to hold court.

'Welcome to Shangri-la,' he boomed, as I stepped ashore.

Behind him, under the flame-trees, stood the Vatuan police band, resplendent in their red and white uniforms. Their drummer began to beat the retreat on a wooden *lali*.

'Arranged for your arrival to coincide with our evening flag-lowering ceremony,' Pennington explained. 'Follow me to the dais,' he whispered, indicating a raised wooden platform beside the flag-pole.

I would have been up there in a jiffy if my judge's knee-breeches had not been braced up to my armpits. Complete with heavy silver buttons, they had me gripped like plaster casts.

'Either get on or off,' said Pennington, 'the flag's half-way down already.'

I had in fact no time to do either. With a clash of cymbals the band broke into the national anthem and I was obliged to make my bow in a somewhat unconventional attitude.

Two grinning bandsmen stepped forward upon Pennington's command. 'At the double now, lads,' he told them. They picked up my law books and other belongings and set off towards an open two-seater parked under the coconut trees.

'I boast the only motor in the islands,' Pennington

informed me. It was an early French model painted in green stripes. 'Specially camouflaged for bird-watching,' he claimed. Pennington folded himself into the front seat. 'Put the Judge in the dicky,' he instructed the bandsmen.

He let out the clutch with a jerk and reversed at high speed along the precipitous coastal track. It struck me as dangerous, but Pennington seemed to know most of the twists in the road. At each corner he blew upon a hunting horn.

'Will it only go backwards?' I inquired after a while. Even on trains, travelling backwards has an unsettling effect on me. 'Do we have to make the whole journey like this?'

'No, no,' he reassured me, 'just for a few miles. It's the only way to loosen up the mesh so that I can use the front gears.'

We stopped at a village where we were presented with tropical fruit and a sucking pig.

'Afraid you'll have to make room for it with you,' said Pennington. I spent the rest of the journey peering anxiously through a grille of bananas with a porker under my scarlet tippet.

Eventually we came to a halt outside a large wooden house overlooking the bay. 'The Residency,' said Pennington. 'Your room is at the side.' My guest suite contained no sign of a bed.

'Don't approve of beds,' he told me, 'most unhealthy. Got rid of them all when Edith went back.' Rumour had it that Pennington's wife had been on long leave since 1922.

Bed or no bed, it was a great relief to be safely indoors and to get out of my hot robes at last. 'Good chance to freshen up,' I decided, making for the ablutions.

'Use the tub at my end,' called Pennington, just in time. One doesn't expect to find a young crocodile in the guest-room bath, even though one's host is a keen naturalist.

I rescued my towel and retreated.

'Feeling all right, old chap?' demanded Pennington as I faltered past.

'Oh yes,' I insisted, 'quite a break in the circuit routine, though.'

After supper, Pennington played his gramophone, the earliest model I had even seen. He had four badly cracked records, all operatic. The first side he tried was unplayable. He turned the record over. 'Now for a bit of *Tosca*,' he announced. I sat politely through 'Elucevan le stelle', the performance of which was lavishly extended whenever the needle stuck.

'I see I'm trying your local witch doctor tomorrow,' I remarked. I was endeavouring to read the case papers in preparation for the next day.

'What for?' he asked, winding away at the gramophone.

'Failing to make rain,' I answered. For once my host was nonplussed.

'Hardly a crime,' he countered.

'It is if you take money from the villagers that way,' I explained. 'Obtaining by false pretences, contrary to the Larceny Ordinance.'

As I spoke, there came a flash of lightning beyond the verandah and then thunder and more lightning. 'Sultry weather,' I said. A cloud-burst almost drowned my comment.

'There goes your case,' laughed Pennington in triumph, as the rain pelted down. 'Some witch doctor, eh? We reckon him the best there is in these parts!'

I pointed out that there were many other counts in the indictment preferred against the wily magician, but he was no longer interested. He gave an enormous yawn and stretched to his full six-and-a-half feet, then picked up a pile of barkcloth and threw it over my arm.

'Time to turn in,' he announced. 'You'll get a far better night's sleep on this than on any of your damned spring mattresses.'

The storm was still raging as I prepared for rest, but my set of the *Laws of England* proved invaluable. Neatly stacked around my head they made an excellent shield against the

appalling draughts that whipped through ever crevice in
the room. The next day dawned fine and sunny.

'Breakfast,' came the roaring summons from the verandah.
I arrived to find my host in an unconventional position.

'Always eat lying on the left side,' he said from the low
charpoy alongside the table. 'Gets the juices racing downhill
from the pancreas into the duodenum.' He was busy
dipping bread and butter soldiers into his sixth boiled egg. 'I
suppose you'll be expecting a bench to sit on!' He slapped
his thigh and was laughing uproariously at his joke, when a
tiny old native appeared, dragging a canvas chair. 'Good
boy, Narle,' approved my host.

'Always keep a chair about the place,' he explained. 'For
self-defence.' It was certainly not kept for comfort, I
discovered. 'Yes, indeed,' he continued, 'when taken
unawares and unarmed, one can always present the chair.
The legs are very confusing to an enraged fanatic.'

In some ways I would have preferred to be confronted by
the fanatic rather than the high bowl of porridge which lay
in wait for me at the table. It was topped with a mound of
grated coconut.

'An unusual combination,' I observed. I trenched out the
nearest corner with my spoon.

'Don't be alarmed by the teeth,' Pennington interjected.

'Sorry?' I said.

'Hadn't you noticed?' he asked.

'Noticed what?'

'My dentures,' he explained. 'Bad fit. Always get that
double click.' He paused. 'Hear it? First, when the molars
lock. Then the gums. Never been the same since my launch
overturned on the Efiti lighthouse reef.'

'I believe Boots the Chemist make a special preparation
for that sort of problem,' I answered. 'Not that it would be
easy to get supplies of that sort as far afield as Vatua, but
when I . . .'

Pennington was not listening to me. He had sprung up
and was seated at what looked like a harmonium at the far

corner of the verandah. 'Came out with the missionaries fifty years ago—still good as new,' he said. 'Always limber up for the day at the keyboard. How about "Dreamy Days on the Lagoon"?' He crashed into a sequence of violent and unrelated chords.

'Don't think I know it,' I called.

'You wouldn't, it's one of mine,' he retorted.

The top of the harmonium was covered with an interesting gallery of shrunken heads and faded photographs. 'Relatives of yours?' I asked.

'Just the pictures,' he replied.

He switched abruptly from symphonic to vamp. Sepia ancestors in Victorian plumes and helmets shimmied along the polished surface to the beat of the Black Bottom. Pennington proceeded to list them from left to right.

'Great Uncle Rufus—Skinner's Horse—lost both ears to a sepoy in the Mutiny; devil's own luck, though—lived to go down on the poop of a sloop in the Bay of Bengal. Left his widow, Aunt Dot, comfortably off, though. Not that you'd have guessed. Terribly mean was Aunt Dot. When she died they found a large sack amongst her belongings. It was labelled PIECES OF STRING TOO SHORT TO BE OF ANY USE.'

He pulled out the Vox Humana and launched into 'Rose Marie, I Love You'. 'That one's Great-Grandfather Haze— commanded a Maori tribe of Royalists. "We always fight naked," the Chief told him—"Mind if I come in my dressing-gown", was great-grandfather's reply. Extraordinary character. Lived to 95. A stick of garlic a day was the secret, according to great-grandfather. How he kept *that* a secret he never said.'

I peered over Pennington's shoulder. 'And who's that?' I said, pointing to a bewhiskered gentleman bulging out of his bush jacket and leopardskin cummerbund.

'My father's cousin, Ralphie Cox,' Pennington said. 'His fame was confined to the billiard room at the Planter's Club. Only man who could get round all four walls without touching the floor. The Human Fly of Fatibahore, they called him. Won a fortune in bets. Spent it all on drink, though. Terrible man for the bottle. Called on a former school chum one day. Poor chap was on his death-bed. "Anything at all I can do for you, old man?" Ralphie asked. "Just remember to pour a bottle of whisky over my grave," was the reply. "Mind if I pass it through my bladder first?" Ralphie wanted to know.'

Narle was now pointedly flicking down the breakfast table with a bundle of dried leaves. 'Office time, master,' he interrupted, pointing to a large Mickey Mouse clock on the sideboard.

'Great Scott, yes,' said Pennington. He bounded up to the Marconi transmitter which stood under his tank of tropical fish, and twirled the knobs.

The familiar chimes from London boomed out the hour—twelve behind ours.

Narle paused reverently in his dusting. 'Big Benny,' he breathed.

'He insists it's the voice of some damned god,' said Pennington.

He picked up a battered Gladstone bag and led the way to the car. He was off for the week on safari to the interior of the island. Narle scampered after us, half-buried in a mountain of mosquito netting.

'Make sure you tuck it well in,' directed Pennington, as the helpful midget fixed the gauzy canopy over the top of the motor. 'The mosquitoes can be malarial where I'm going,' he explained, 'so I like to play it safe.'

It took Narle some minutes to drape the vehicle to his master's satisfaction, but at least this time there was no trouble with the gear box, and we set off normally enough. Although from my place in the dicky, the view through the mesh was necessarily hazy.

As we approached a village, old men and children ran for shelter at the sight of the phantom vehicle bearing down on them out of the forest. 'You'd think they'd be used to it by now,' complained Pennington. 'It must be the sight of a stranger.'

He flashed an irritable look at me over his shoulder. 'What on earth are you doing up there?' he demanded.

'The only way to get my robe box in the dicky was to sit on it,' I replied.

'Well, at least you could put your umbrella down,' he expostulated. 'After last night's downpour we won't get rain again for weeks.'

It seemed neither the time nor the place to explain my old problem with sunburn, which was one of my continual crosses in the tropics. Anyway, we had arrived at the courthouse.

'Do try to cut out the eccentricities, old boy,' said Pennington, clamping my shoulder in a fatherly fashion. 'The white man on his own has to be a bit of a conformist or he goes all to pot.'

He nipped back under his white canopy. 'Best of luck,' he called. 'Until we meet again.' With a farewell toot of the hunting horn, he floated off into the distance like the bridal procession from *Lohengrin*.

After Pennington's departure, I continued to billet at his house until the Session was concluded. Narle did his best to brighten up my evenings by producing a black-and-gold tin of Harrogate Toffees after dinner. 'Master's Lollies,' he would explain, rationing me to a selection of two on each occasion.

My work at court, which ended that first visit to the South Island of Vatua, concerned a boring matter of pasturing rights. All in all it was an anticlimax after my extraordinary introduction to island life *à la* Pennington.

Looking back to those years, I find it difficult to believe that such characters as Pennington ever existed. But he was only one of several. Years of service in torrid climates, accentuated by isolation from conventional society, may be some sort of explanation.

All Commissioners in the South Pacific were empowered

to make local bye-laws under various Statutes, in matters of Health, Public Works, Development, and so on. It was part of the job of the visiting Judge to check upon such regulations. Occasionally the Judge might have to declare bye-laws or regulations *ultra vires*, as lawyers say; to pronounce, in other words, that the Commissioner had exceeded his powers—'an excess of jurisdiction', in legal language.

Pennington, I was to learn upon subsequent visits, had made some pretty odd regulations. Nothing, however, compared with what my predecessor, Judge Donaldson, had encountered when he visited Tunafola, in the time of Commissioner Macnab.

15

An Excess of Jurisdiction

For Duncan Macnab, as Rory Donaldson dryly observed, slumber had never been more sweet than toil. The newly appointed District-Commissioner of Tunafola did not approve of any land in which it always seemed afternoon. Tennyson's poem 'The Lotus Eaters' meant little to this remarkable Colonial Administrative Officer from Perthshire.

His fellow Scot, Robert Louis Stevenson, thought Tunafola the most beautiful of the coral islands. Stevenson wrote of 'nights of a heavenly brightness, and the clash of the surf on the reef'.

Duncan Macnab was unimpressed. All he noted was that 'the men of the island could spear fish, climb palm-trees, grow taro, and make bonito hooks. If they felt like it. They rarely did.' Macnab himself was a man who snapped out of bed at dawn. He was the only European on the island, but far too busy to notice any lack of companionship. Within two months of his arrival, the Commissioner had filled his tiny thatched office on the headland with bamboo filing-cabinets to hold an ever-increasing number of draft bye-laws.

'Development Regulations,' he called them. The bulky folders contained in earnest detail such subjects as Fishing Grounds, Timber Cutting, Mining Prospects, Land Conservation, Co-operative Farming, Insect Pest Clearance, and the Destruction of Noxious Weeds. He frequently addressed the elders in the tribal meeting house, after swallowing, with some impatience, the customary offering of *savasava*, a local toddy, drunk on official occasions.

'You can't just lie about waiting for the coconuts to fall,' he remonstrated.

'But we don't,' they replied politely. 'That is the duty of our women-folk.'

The commissioner threw up his fists in despair. 'A murrain on your women-folk,' he fulminated. 'They could well set you a better example.'

Regrettably, the women of Tunafola were renowned not for their industry but for their looks. They spent their time eating mangoes, combing their hair, and making love whenever possible, which was always.

Some weeks after his arrival, the Commissioner was working late at his Development Regulations wrapped in a heavy plaid dressing-gown, when a sudden wind blew out the oil lamp. 'Drat,' he exclaimed, springing up to relight it—a task which was never completed. The next moment the lamp itself had crashed to the ground, and the sudden wind was a howling gale.

The privilege of living on the most elevated site on the island had its snags, especially during the hurricane season. By the time the cyclone had passed over, Duncan Macnab was without a house. His office, too, had gone, and his filing cabinets. Apart from a few books, he had lost all his Development Regulations. This was bad enough. What was far, far worse was that he could not replace them. The storm had destroyed every scrap of paper he possessed, along with his writing equipment.

For three days, he paced desperately up and down the white sands. He could think of no work to do.

On the afternoon of the fourth day, he was obsessively clipping his oleander bushes into neat ornamental shapes with a surviving pair of office scissors, when inspiration came.

What was the Tunafolans' only fault? he asked himself. The answer was simple: indolence. Hereditary indolence. He dropped the scissors with a start. Why in heaven had the idea not occurred to him before? New blood must be introduced. The race must be crossed with a breed renowned for its industry—the breed of the Macnabs!

The Resident Commissioner removed his kilt and plunged into the lagoon. Back on shore, he stood shaking the water off his tall frame. He was built like a Lanark pine. 'Macnab', he said, slipping back into his sporran, 'your duty's clear.' Ever a stickler for tradition, he tucked the hibiscus flower of courtship behind his ear and strode purposefully towards the village.

It was during his first Michaelmas tour of the Circuit that Rory Donaldson paid un unsolicited call on Macnab in Tunafola. There, over a bottle of gin, the Commissioner recounted to the bewildered Judge how he had set out 'to beget with child', as he phrased it, the entire female population of the island.

'Drunken ramblings', was of course the Judge's first assumption. Gradually, however, as the incredible details were confirmed, it became apparent that the Commissioner was telling no less than the truth.

The Population Development Regulation, Schedule A, was the master-file number given by Duncan Macnab to his extraordinary undertaking. To this project he had solemnly dedicated himself—'without fear or favour, prejudice or ill-will', as he noted in his files, recalling the oath he had sworn upon assuming office.

The first step was to obtain the approval of the elders.

At an emergency session in the meeting house, the Commissioner explained the unique properties of Scottish stock. 'Particularly,' he emphasised, 'in one whose ancestors, on all sides, produced fine families even by Victorian standards.'

Schedule A was surprisingly well received. Apart from certain ladies, exempt by marriage or age, the elders had no objection. But did the Commissioner appreciate, they inquired delicately, that there were nearly 70 eligible partners? No doubt the men of Scotland were of god-like strength, nevertheless.

'First things first, gentlemen,' demurred the Resident Commissioner gruffly. 'I shall get down to detailed regulations later.'

He had already mapped out an 'agenda' on the sandy floor. 'Stage 1' he had written, using a pointed guava stick: 'Exposition'. 'Stage 2: Organisation'. 'Stage 3: Implementation'.

News of Schedule A soon spread among the excited ladies of the island. Some of the more forward began to leave garlands of jasmine in the Commissioner's *bure*. These were not acknowledged.

The Resident Commissioner was entirely preoccupied with 'Stage 2'. His future offspring, he had decided, must be suitably educated. He conducted classes, through his bemused interpreter, in porridge and haggis making. He gave lessons in Scottish history. 'William Wallace,' he told the simpering class, 'was a great Scots leader. He defeated the English at Stirling Bridge in 1297.'

There was only one point of Scottish legend in which the girls were interested. 'Beneath his fine red and green skirt, was Mista Macnab clothed or unclothed?' The Commissioner, a strict Presbyterian, was unamused.

He had, of course, no misgivings whatsoever about the morality of the Plan. Duncan Macnab was well versed in the Scriptures. Jacob, like himself, had dwelt in a strange land—the land of Canaan. The Lord had said unto Jacob: 'Be fruitful and multiply.' Jacob, he recalled, had acted upon this advice with a surprising number of hand-maidens. Hence the twelve tribes of Israel.

Stage 3 of Schedule A was to begin with the full moon. At this juncture the Commissioner could no longer afford to ignore the offerings of jasmine. The largest bunches came from Mathilda, daughter of the leading elder. She was determined to have pride of place among the Commissioner's brides. This was now agreed and preparations set in hand.

'Have I forgotten anything?' pondered the Commissioner,

his mind a vast compendium of largely irrelevant data. 'No,' he finally concluded, 'I think not. All that remains is the, er, implementation.'

For probably the first time in his life, Duncan Macnab found himself faltering. The reason can be easily guessed. So far as ladies were concerned the Resident Commissioner of Tunafola was no man of the world. True, there had been one romantic episode in his life.

He had once gone beagling, alone, with Flora Reid, a strapping girl of noble birth from Inverness, who married into the Finnish aristocracy. But experience rather than romance was what Macnab stood in need of, at this crisis of his life, on a lonely island, eleven and a half degrees north of Capricorn.

The rituals accompanying his initial assignation were in themselves unnerving. In Tunafola, the traditional bridal suite was a canoe, seven feet long, and of the finest wood, decorated with stained sinnet and cowrie shells. The wedding feast was followed by a six-hour song and dance ritual known as the *aloa meke*. This lasted well into the evening.

Eventually, bedecked in flowers, Duncan Macnab and his bride were laid ceremonially on the nuptial litter in the centre of the canoe. Mounds of sweet potato, bananas and coconuts were piled around them. 'Even lovers must eat,' cackled the matrons of honour, pushing them adrift. Along the shore the moonlight glinted on the palm fronds.

'We're painfully cramped in here,' protested the Commissioner, as the narrow craft lurched out on the ebb tide.

Forty-eight hours later the islanders were out again to greet him with further dancing as he paddled ashore by the morning light, triumphant if sea-sick.

During the following months, partner succeeded partner in the bridal canoe. It was not until the end of the year that it occurred to the Commissioner that something might be wrong. He decided to confer in secret with the elders.

Had they learnt of any results? he inquired. Their intelligence system, he knew, was foolproof. No, they reported sadly, the first signs of the Harvest had yet to appear. The Commissioner was disappointed. However, the tale of Robert the Bruce and the spider had always impressed him. He was not a man who gave up easily.

Rarely can an officer of the Crown have worked with such devotion to the Imperial Service. Or with so little success. Yet he would not admit defeat.

He redoubled his breathing exercises and flung himself desperately into a fresh programme.

All without avail.

The Commissioner began to walk like a man repeatedly struck by lightning.

It was in this sad state that Judge Donaldson found him. And, to the Judge, he poured out the whole story, confirming every extraordinary detail by referring to the inhabitants of the island.

The Judge lost no time in pronouncing Schedule A 'and all proposed regulations pertaining thereto—*ultra vires*'. He also ensured that the Commissioner was quickly retired. Duncan Macnab ended his days in Bournemouth, haunted by what he considered an inexplicable failure.

It was left to Judge Donaldson, in the course of a protracted enquiry, to provide an answer. As the Judge noted, on page 34 of his report, the probable explanation for the failure of Macnab's Schedule A was a botanical one. There grew on the island of Tunafola a vine-like creeper known as *Desmodium dependens blume*. When boiled, this plant produced a juice known as *savasava*. *Savasava* was often reserved by the Tunafolans for persons of great distinction. 'The impressive dignity of its formal presentation,' wrote Donaldson, 'cannot fail to engender a feeling of pride in the honoured recipient.'

'*Savasava*,' he proceeded, 'also induces temporary sterility, a fact unknown to the Tunafolans in those early years, but undoubtedly the reason, also, for the extraordinary degree of population control in these tiny atolls.'

From every point of view, the Judge concluded, Commissioner Macnab had clearly exceeded his powers.

16

The Weight of the Law

A few weeks after my return to base from Vatua, I received an unexpected summons to go back there.

'Need you urgently on North Island,' read the message from Pennington. 'Tribal problems at Nasoro. Must be settled without delay.'

I managed to get across in record time, on a Sunderland flying-boat.

The ANZAC pilot brought me safely down into the Nasoro lagoon, where Pennington was waiting in his launch to take me ashore.

'Had exactly the same trouble when Rory Donaldson was Circuit Judge,' he explained, upon greeting me aboard the plane. 'But of course he was ready-made for the job.'

'Was he indeed?' I replied, piqued. 'I hope I can hold a judicial inquiry as well as my predecessor.'

'Don't doubt it,' said Pennington. 'The point is that Donaldson was at least twice your size.'

He stooped down and helped to free me. I seemed to have parcelled myself up rather too securely with the extra length of seat-belt.

'You must be the skinniest judge in the world,' he reflected. 'Steady on,' I said, 'the weight of judicial authority isn't measured in crude physical terms.'

Pennington continued to stroke his beaky nose in gloomy contemplation. 'Obviously nobody's told you about the Nasoro people,' he said.

This was true. There had been no time to obtain a preliminary briefing before setting out.

'Authority is measured in weight here,' explained Pennington. 'Weight and strength. It's as simple as that. Unfortunately you fail in both departments.'

I pulled down my wigbox from the luggage rack and began to shake out my judge's gown, after tying on my collar bands.

Pennington picked up an inflatable life-jacket. 'Could you perhaps wear this under your gown,' he suggested.

'But it's only fifty yards to the beach,' I said. I peered through the aircraft window at the glassy blue sea. 'Still, if you think one shouldn't take the risk . . .'

'Not at all, old man,' laughed Pennington. 'I merely thought it might help to fill you out a bit!'

His jocular remarks had now focused the attention of the pilot and the other members of the crew on to me, just as I was trying to get into my gown. A sudden gust of wind through the open hatch had somehow got the sleeves entangled with the overhead breathing apparatus.

'Dracula lives,' sniggered one of the crew, from the cockpit door.

'The Phantom of the Lagoon,' rejoined his assistant. They guffawed together in their rough Antipodean way.

I snapped myself free and turned to Pennington. 'The sooner we get ashore, the better,' I said.

'I'll take you straight to the Rest House,' he told me. 'We'll have a serious pow-wow once we're there.'

The Rest House, a ramshackle bungalow overlooking the bay, had been stocked with provisions for my stay. Pennington joined me for a sundowner on the verandah.

'There's what all the trouble's about.' He pointed to a sandy atoll lying 200 years beyond the reef. 'Nasoro Bay,' he continued, 'is famous for underwater volcanic activity. Every so often, it throws up an atoll like that one.' Pennington helped himself to another large glass of whisky.

'That's when Nasoro needs a visit from the Circuit Judge, d'y'see, to decide title to one of the new bits of land that suddenly appears.' He drained his glass. 'As I say, the last occasion was in Rory Donaldson's time.'

A cool breeze had sprung up. Pennington draped himself in a tattered hide shawl. 'Always the same trouble with a whisky bottle,' he complained, shaking out the last drop, 'too much for one, not enough for two.' Since he'd consumed nearly all of it himself, I said nothing.

'Why do the Nasoro tribes squabble so fiercely over one atoll?' I asked.

'Turtles,' said Pennington. He settled back with a cheroot. 'Turtles are the wariest of all creatures in these waters,' he expounded. 'When they sun themselves on the reef they know that the rising tide will keep them secure from enemies. When they do the same thing on the new atoll, thinking it's the reef, they are left stranded.' He flapped his mosquito boots in a vivid demonstration of helpless flippers. 'That's when the blighters are caught by the islanders. In hundreds. Very precious they are, too. And the fighting starts as to who they actually belong to.'

He got up and started rummaging amongst the stores for a fresh supply of liquor. 'Do they always beat their drums so loudly?' I inquired. The Rest House was at least a mile from the nearest village but the noise of the wooden drums was considerable.

'Quite frankly,' declared Pennington, returning with some brandy, 'the rival factions here are working themselves up into a frenzy over the business.' He poured himself a tumbler of brandy.

'Where do you suggest I hold the Inquiry?' I asked. 'That's the danger,' said Pennington. 'You'll have to hold it out of doors. No building on Nasoro will hold the crowds. Hope they don't get out of hand with you. Could be nasty.'

I took a quick sip at my drink. 'Of course they'd never have gone for Donaldson,' said Pennington. 'Built like an oak tree, d'y'see. Just what the islanders respect.'

We shared a simple meal of tinned bully-beef. 'On a diet or something?' asked Pennington, as I toyed with my food.

'Just digestive problems,' I replied. 'Try to keep off rich foods.'

'Well you could at least try an extra yam with your meals,' he went on, 'nothing rich about that,' I nodded. In a moment he reappeared from the kitchen with a vegetable the size of a rugby ball.

'Just one of these a day could do wonders,' he said.

'What *is* all this business about building the physique, this constant emphasis on weight, over here?' I demanded irritably. I was tired of slurs and determined to thrash the thing out.

'The tradition among the people,' explained Pennington, 'is that they're descended from a race of giants. I can show you a row of eight-foot-high stones that they say represent their early ancestors. They do their best to live up to them today—massive intakes of food, ancient body-building techniques and so on.' He bunched his shoulders playfully. 'so the news is, Sunny Jim, "in Nasoro, BIG IS BEAUTI-FUL".' Pennington prided himself on his unconvincing American gangster imitations.

Once I had seen Pennington off the premises I decided to get down to some legal research. 'Whatever Donaldson might have had over me in weight,' I resolved, 'I'll try to make up for in the old brain work.'

There was in any event no hope of a peaceful night's sleep. The drumming seemed to be getting even louder, but I blotted it out with a few solid hours mugging up over books and papers.

I must have fallen asleep over them, for I woke to find my head pillowed between Halsbury's *Volume VI* on *Damages* and *Volume XII* on *Torts*. Despite a bit of a hangover, I was dressed and ready for action when Pennington arrived next morning.

'Have had to postpone the hearing,' he called from the path. I suppose I had been too tensed up for the ordeal ahead to notice that torrential rain was falling.

'Can't do anything until the weather improves.' He

tethered his horse to the verandah rail and hurried inside.
'Why on earth have you got all these books in your bed?' he
demanded. I hastily dismantled my nocturnal library.

'Working on the legal side of the problem,' I said.
Pennington marched through into the kitchen and flung
off his hide wrap. He had an armful of under-ripe mangoes
which he began to munch with relish.

'Did you feel that earth tremor in the night?' he asked as I
joined him at the breakfast table, where he was dipping his
mangoes into a mixture of curry powder and vinegar. I
explained that I had been too preoccupied to notice anything of that sort.

'Nothing to worry about,' he reassured me. 'We do get
them from time to time. Now to work.' He produced a
pencil stub from behind one hairy ear and began to sketch
on the whitewashed wall beside us.

'Had an idea!' he announced. He drew a large rectangle.
'This is the clearing in the principal village where you'll be
holding court,' he began. He etched in the surrounding
bures. 'There are two tall coconut trees—here,' he marked
a cross at the top of his rectangle, 'and here.' He made
another cross.

'Now if I get a sort of bamboo platform slung very high
between these two trees,' he went on 'would you mind
adjudicating from up there?' He began to sketch out a
rough design.

'A really lofty perch could be very impressive,' he
enthused. 'And what's more—safe! Far above the madding
crowd and so on.' He turned enthusiastically towards me. I
shrank slightly. There were moments when I really felt
that mentally Pennington, like Macnab, was almost a
borderline case. One could only humour him at such times.

'An interesting arrangement,' I said. 'Only thing, I
couldn't hear anything—what with the wind and so on.'

Pennington split open a coconut and drank from it
thoughtfully. 'As you please,' he said. 'Personally, I rather
like the idea of crow's nest justice!'

'I think it's straining the adaptability of the legal system,' I continued firmly. 'As for the madding crowd, I hope I can rely on your control of the situation there.'

I pulled back the curtain of sailcloth from the kitchen window and peered out. The rain was still pelting down. Pennington got up to leave. 'I'll be back when the weather clears,' he announced. He looked down gloomily at my bowl of Branlax and surrounding circle of vitamin pills. 'We can only hope for the best,' he said.

It continued to rain throughout that day. I pursued my studies in the kitchen but to little effect. The English law of real property, so far as I could see, had little to say about Melanesian atolls. It was a gap I was about to fill, I trusted.

'A Note on the Law Relating to Volcanic Eruptions'. I rolled the title in my mind. It was an exciting thought. I was dreaming about it that night, in fact, when I was suddenly turned out of my charpoy by a very noticeable earthquake. The finger of destiny, I reflected, climbing back again. My treatise must certainly cover subterranean tremors, I thought. However, there were no other shocks and, dog-tired, I fell asleep once more.

The morning was bright and clear. All seemed peaceful in the village with not a drumbeat to be heard. I ventured out on to the shore. The scent of jasmine, pandanus and frangipani mingled delightfully with the salt of the sea. The waves of the reef stretched unbroken across the horizon. But where was the controversial atoll?

'Seem to have lost my sense of direction,' I murmured. 'Could have sworn that was where Pennington pointed it out.' I swivelled around. Looked left. Looked right. Then it began to dawn on me.

'Goodness me,' I exclaimed at last, 'it's disappeared.' There was no doubt about it. 'Must have been the earthquake in the night! And now it has disintegrated back into the depths again!'

'I was still adjusting myself to this extraordinary

example of the unwritten laws of the natural world when I saw Pennington galloping up towards me. Before he could dismount, I was greeting him with the news. 'Last night's quake,' I called out. 'It's put paid to your atoll.' He waved his hunting horn in my direction and dismounted.

'Can't hear you,' he said. I repeated the information. 'It's no good,' he said, shaking his head like a large dog. 'Got this blasted humming in my ears. My mother told me it was the 'cello. She took it up during pregnancy, d'you see?'

'The earthquake,' I bellowed.

'Yes, that's what brings it on,' he agreed, hearing me at last. 'Always does.'

'The atoll,' I shouted, 'it's gone!'

'Bless my soul,' he said, 'so it has.' He began to laugh. 'At least it didn't take you with it.' He clapped a hand on my shoulder. I was only too pleased to share his merriment. Together, we made doubly sure that the atoll had gone for good, and Pennington set off to transmit a radio message to the Royal New Zealand Air Force Station in Samoa.

'They'll send over a Sunderland to pick you up tomorrow evening,' he reported later in the day. 'After all, not much point in your hanging on here. Looks as if your case has been settled out of court. Divine intervention, you might call it.'

We took a stroll through the feathery pampas grass. The fruit bats peered down with interest from their upside-down perches in the banyan trees. I began almost to regret having to leave such an unspoilt haven of tropical flora and fauna.

'Seems a pity to slip away so quickly,' I said.

'Not exactly slipping away,' rejoined Pennington. 'There's a tribal farewell in your honour tomorrow afternoon.'

'A friendly one, I trust,' I said. 'After all, I've hardly put on much muscle in twenty-four hours.'

'Ah,' said Pennington, 'but the people now associate you with the Great Earthquake. It's the biggest they've known and your arrival is obviously the reason for it in their eyes.

Given you a kind of new status. Magical rather than physical, of course.'

Now that I was no longer required to sit in judgement, I rather looked forward to my meeting with the people.

The following day, a half-circle of warriors, huge men in *tarpa* and warpaint, awaited our arrival on the sandy slope leading into the principal village. In front of them was a large pit filled with stones. Closer to, I could see they had been heated by burning charcoal to a sizzling temperature.

'Cooking ovens?' I suggested.

'Curtain raiser, actually,' said Pennington. 'You'll see. We sit here,' he directed, indicating a flowered canopy at the summit. Around us the solemn tribesmen chanted their approval.

'Take your wig off,' whispered Pennington. 'They want to make you an offering.' Their emissaries discharged a pungent bowl of sacred oil over my head. 'Shows you've earned tremendous respect,' said Pennington.

'I'd never have guessed,' I quipped gamely, mopping the surplus out of my ears.

'And now the fire-walk,' said Pennington, indicating the smoking pit. I looked down anxiously at my buckled shoes.

'It's not going to do these much good,' I fenced.

'No, no,' he chuckled. 'This is their show. The young braves have to walk across to prove their manhood to you.'

Green leaves had been thrown across the stones. Over the fiercely hissing arena, a troupe of brawny youths romped to and fro with shouts of triumph.

The performance over, the twenty-four athletes lined up and marched towards me. 'They want you to examine their feet,' Pennington explained.

'Chiropody's not exactly my line,' I cringed. 'We'll take that as read. Formal evidence not required.'

At a signal from the Chief, the young men dispersed. Formal speeches followed, and the presentation of bread-fruit, rolled in ritual fashion across the green. I also received a Nasoro fan, of black and white cock's feathers.

This had been fashioned for the occasion by the island schoolchildren. When their headmaster bent to give it to me, he seized the opportunity to whisper something in my ear.

'Wants to know if nature's calling,' Pennington translated.

It was a welcome suggestion. Together Pennington and I made our way to where a small building covered with cowrie shells and painted barkcloth had been specially erected for the occasion. I peered inside. It was a rather unusual closet designed to accommodate both of us. The entire construction was embowered in dried seaweed.

'Yours is the one with the Union Jack,' said Pennington.

On our return, they were preparing for the dancing. The gentlemen of the band were flourishing their nose pipes.

'Here come the girls,' said Pennington, as a scrummage of enormous ladies, with hibiscus in their hair, descended on me. I had a premonition that each muscular arm would make four of mine..

'You'd better get rid of your Western ideas of beauty,' laughed Pennington.

The dance itself was a sort of rock 'n' roll cum samba. I was picked up by the leader like some sort of mascot. Soon it took on the nightmarish quality of an Amazonian excuse-me.

Pennington seemed totally unaware of my ordeal. 'You're obviously a big hit with the ladies,' he called as I whirled past, like an odd sock caught up in a washing machine.

Never before have I been more pleased to hear the drone of an aircraft. The RNZAF Sunderland had landed on the lagoon, and the dance was abandoned as everyone crowded out to meet it. I found myself pushed along to the fore.

'Here he is,' called Pennington to the New Zealand Air Force officer awaiting me in a dinghy as I hobbled towards the water's edge. 'The Maker of Earthquakes.'

'He certainly looks as if he's been in a few,' said the

aviator, a more sympathetic specimen than his colleague on the outward flight.

'It's not the earthquakes' I explained. 'It's the Trojan women.'

'Bit of a new experience for a Judge, eh?' said the officer.

'Oh, I don't know,' I said, as we roared off, 'there was a chap called Breveton in the Middle Ages.'

'Who was he, then?' he asked.

I reached for my set of Halsbury, bundled safely aboard by Pennington. 'If you're really interested,' I said, turning up the reference, 'it was recorded in this early report of 1333.'

I began to read the extract.

'Hugo de Breveton was Edward the Third's Justiciary at the January Azzize in the Wrekin.' Apparently he had dealt out some heavy sentences on the menfolk of the region and the wives took revenge on him.

'Hys Eminence,' reported the Chronicler, 'was fulle sore wracked by ye feerce and mightie Jezebels.'

The flying-boat straightened out as we set off for home.

'And how are you feeling now?' asked the kindly New Zealand aviator. 'Sore wracked,' I said, reaching into my travel-pack for Dr Grimshaw's Medicinal Spirits.

A couple of swigs rapidly anaesthetised the system, putting me into a reflective mood. As we roared through the sky above the shoals of Oceania, I found myself contrasting in my mind the uninhibited ladies of the South Seas with their purdah-veiled sisters whom I had encountered when on the Bench in British Arabia.

17

A Sympathetic Hearing

The ship's bell hanging in the Great Breadfruit Tree on the island of Guala, tolled nine.

'Oyez, Oyez, Oyez,' called the Court Inspector, tightening his loincloth as he stepped into the island long-house, a court-setting familiar to me out in the South Seas.

Regretfully, I laid aside my three-month-old copy of the *Airmail Times*. I had just embarked on the Correspondence Page. Councillor Goodenough, Chairman of the Borstal After Care Committee, had written a strong letter to the Editor. He was complaining of a 'total breakdown of communication' between the fuddy-duddies on the Bench' and 'youth everywhere'. I should have liked to read on, but I had to get on with the work in hand. A hotly contested prosecution of four teenagers for netting Tahitian Whitebait by night, without a warning flare, occupied the whole of the day. The trial ended with an acquittal.

The tropical night had fallen by the time I was able to slip into my canvas safari-bath. I was due to attend an island function that night, so I changed into evening mufti and hurried out to the village clearing.

I was guest of honour at something called the Guundulu Thanksgiving, a tribal ceremony about which I was somewhat vague.

'Hors d'oeuvre?' I asked the Inspector as a large blob of something fishy was placed in front of me.

'Guundulu,' explained the Inspector who was seated alongside. 'Sacred Sea-Slug.'

'Anything to wash it down with? I suggested. The

Inspector handed me a wooden beaker. 'Toddy wine,' he explained.

I should have been more cautious. But I had to drown the Guundulu in something.

At first I hardly realised the effect of the wine. I can vaguely recollect a party of elders inviting me to participate in some sort of initiation ceremony. It was the kind of thing one often encountered in Micronesia—endless speeches and chanting while the drums went on and on. I'm afraid I fell asleep half-way through.

'Morning, lordship.' The Inspector was bending over me with my breakfast pineapple.

I looked up bleary-eyed. The islanders seemed to have put me to bed on a pile of mats.

'Prefer to wash and shave first, officer,' I said. He produced my sponge bag and a large bowl of water. 'A bit of morning-after,' I said, putting my hand to my head.

I sat up with a jerk. 'Great Heavens!' A cold sweat broke out as I rummaged frantically in my bag. The shaving mirror showed all. My head had been shorn and tattooed.

'Sinnet juice,' explained the Inspector. 'Now Your Lordship is God of the Guundulu for always.'

'Always!' I repeated. I applied my flannel to the more virulent patches, but soap was to no avail against the art of the tribal elders.

I turned to my pineapple. Glancing again in the mirror, it seemed we had something in common. I also had a single green tuft adorning my summit. An unnerving thought struck me—my forthcoming travel schedule! I had agreed to stand in for an old friend, Stipendiary R.H. Fitzallen—of New Zealand—in three days' time. A seaplane was to call at the island the following day to take me on the first leg of the journey.

Twenty-four hours did little to improve my appearance. At the last minute, an emergency measure dawned upon me. There were expressions of interest, I must confess, as I boarded the plane, but I ignored them.

A full-bottomed wig and robe is hardly the most comfortable outfit for a tropical flight, although there was really no alternative.

By the time we landed in Samoa I was feeling rather jaded. I had to be an overnight guest at the Residency there. Mrs Bothwick-Lawrence, the Resident's wife, was at the barrier to greet me.

'I'm sure you're longing to get out of all that,' she said nervously, as we swerved up the Residency drive. 'How about a dip in the pool? I've arranged a barbeque lunch. Just a few friends.'

I hastened up the stairs in the wake of the bearer. 'I wonder if you could lend me a bathing cap,' I called down to my hostess from the bedroom window.

Mrs Bothwick-Lawrence laughed disbelievingly. 'A *what*?'

'Afraid I've been having a little scalp trouble,' I shouted back.

There was a hasty conference among the ladies. The next minute the bearer's arm came round the door. I was handed Mrs Bothwick-Lawrence's shower-cap.

I would have preferred one without the polka dots and lace frills—especially when I entered the gentlemen's changing pavilion. I stepped out of my bathing robe.

'Pommie poofter,' grunted the red-faced manager of the local sugar mill, diving in behind me. Someone else spurted a can of Foster's lager in my direction, as I floated away on a Lilo.

The rest of the day I spent in bed, my head swathed in a muslin shawl. 'Doctor's orders,' I explained to my hostess.

Next morning I conducted a close examination of developments. A slight stubble was emerging around the tuft, but the green dye was still predominant. I managed to conceal both conditions under a panama hat I had found on top of the wardrobe. I kept it on throughout the resumed flight.

Just as we were about to land, our stewardess gave us a

warning. Apparently some young people were rioting over a visiting pop group. I decided to keep a low profile.

The airport staff were doing their best to deal with the mob. But in the mêlée my hat was knocked off.

'Kindly remove your grip,' I protested to the chief security officer. His gaze remained fixed on my tribal haircut.

'Why don't you grow up?' he asked. 'These other rockers are half your age!'

It was only by producing my bank-card that I was able to get sense into him. Naturally he was full of apologies as he showed me to the official car.

Then, by one of those extraordinary tricks of fate, the youthful demonstrators were brought up before me in court next morning. My sentencing was a source of comment in the evening papers.

'Sympathy and humanity shown by visiting Judge,' ran the editorial.

It occurred to me that Councillor Goodenough should perhaps have extended his inquiry to the Southern Hemisphere! I re-read his letter on the flight back to Fulala. There was other correspondence in *The Times* on the same subject. A retired Colonial Service Officer, J.M. Watson, OBE, wrote from 'Somali Cot', Budleigh Salterton: 'We should address our minds, in the UK, to the more general issue of the "gap" between the governing and the governed. Bridging that "gap" by a true understanding of local conditions was what I and my colleagues in the British Trust Territories tried to do.'

My own experience confirmed what Mr Watson said. In my travels about the circuit, I encountered many Administrators dedicated to 'understanding' the island folk under their care. Their enthusiasm could even prove startling on occasions.

18

Dyspepsia at Government House

'Baked yowl, fried in gung,' said His Excellency. 'I trust you like our native food?'

'Oh yes, sir,' I growled, my teeth locked in the gung. I was a guest at Government House, in the British Sheba Isles, on the western perimeter of my circuit.

'Can't understand people working out here who eat only English dishes,' he said, 'when there are so many native delicacies to hand.'

A sauce bowl was lowered past my ear. 'Don't be afraid of it,' called HE, as the bearer swamped my plate in green foam. 'It's an island relish, very palatable.'

There was a rattling at my side. It came from the throat of a fellow guest who had just tasted the relish. Kindly servants soon helped him from the table. I bit savagely into a slice of yowl.

'Your trials all going smoothly this trip?' inquired the island Commissioner of Police.

'Up until now,' I replied through my tears. 'Try the salad,' cried the Governor.

'Tropical nettles,' warned the Police Chief, too late.

'English wives with their baked custards, they lost us India,' declared His Excellency. 'There's no colour bar where we all eat the same food.'

The Governor signalled and six servants filed out onto the lawn. They carried towels. 'Just digging out the earth ovens,' he explained. The servants began work, engulfed in flame. Smoke filled the dining-room.

'So delightfully British,' remarked the American wife of an Anglican bishop. The bishop choked discreetly into his handkerchief. 'I just loved that yowl,' said his wife, through the haze.

Outside, excavations were proceeding briskly. The six bearers padded back inside. They carried a tureen emblazoned with the royal coat of arms. There was a flash as the Governor uncovered the tureen. He beamed over the molten black flesh.

'Now, you roll the meat into a ball with the thumb and forefinger, thus,' he demonstrated. We rolled our meat balls on the Wedgwood dinner service.

'There's jolly well no lack of vitamins in this, sir,' said a visiting anthropologist, between spasms.

'That's why the people in these parts are so robust,' replied His Excellency.

The native band on the terrace was playing selections from *Oklahoma*. 'Ever see the show?' asked the Governor's ADC.

'No,' I muttered, slipping another lump of yowl upon the ledge under the table.

'Have a glass of root cup,' said His Excellency.

'I'll stick to the solids if you don't mind, sir,' I demurred, stabbing another forkful of grey sludge. 'I suppose one gets to like these exotic dishes,' I murmured to my neighbour, the District Officer.

'Never,' he sighed, in silent mastication, 'but I don't want to lose my job.'

'A remarkable fruit,' proclaimed the Governor, as we began the dessert. 'Just eat the pips, leave the rest,' he warned, 'it's poisonous. You'll find the pips simply delicious, but do first scrape them clean.'

We got through the fruit with only one casualty, a bearded Sikh at the end of the table who proved a careless scraper.

'Ladies and Gentlemen, the Sovereign,' boomed the Governor, above the sound of my hiccoughs. He took me by surprise. I was hunched over my finger-bowl, drinking water from the wrong side.

'Such a cute way to drink the loyal toast,' cried the bishop's wife admiringly. The ladies hurried away.

'Gather round, gentlemen, commanded the Governor. We formed a flatulent circle about him. 'Did you know the islanders smoke their own version of the hookah?' he said with pride. His Excellency indicated a pile of bladders and bamboo-piping at his feet. The bladders gurgled sullenly. 'Don't inhale too much,' he cautioned, passing the mouth-piece to the bishop.

'Very fragrant,' gasped the bishop, ashen-faced. A village choir began to sing for us under the candelabra.

The Governor unstoppered a decanter. 'Try our man-grove liqueur,' he urged, savouring the bouquet. 'They brew it in the swamp, you know.' We held back, appalled by its malicious orange colour. The Governor drank steadily. At last he spoke. 'Shall we join the ladies?' he said.

We helped each other on to the terrace. I searched Government House for an empty bathroom but all nine were occupied. When I returned, the stronger guests had begun to leave. The Governor shook my hand.

'Just a minute, Judge,' he said, while a bearer stowed a covered basket in the boot of my car.

'HE never sends a guest away without a little gift.' whispered the ADC.

'What's in it?' I asked, deeply touched.

'Only two dozen yowl and a bag of gung,' smiled the ADC as I ricocheted away.

Next morning my court Registrar kindly relieved me of the yowl. He parcelled it out to thirty-four of his wife's relations. The gung he kept for himself.

The South Sea Islands seemed to me to inspire their British Administrators with an especial zeal to adopt local customs. And not merely in matters of food. Sir Edward Warburton had antimacassars of bark-cloth affixed to every Waring and Gillow chair of the State Drawing-Room. In the principal guest suite, Sir Howard Bartle substituted log-shaped wooden headrests for pillows—the kind favoured by the Melanesian Bigheads to preserve their elaborate hair-styles. The boom of hide war-drums summoned guests to breakfast under the regime of Sir Rigby and Lady Saunders. Sir Hugh Wyn-Roberts became an adept on the Tongan nose flute, much to the dismay of his captive audiences at Vice Regal musical evenings.

Sir Arthur Gordon, an early Governor of the Western Pacific, always trod the island barefoot, in native fashion. His officials were requested to do the same. However, his fondness for the island way of life firmly excluded one particular Polynesian practice. This was the softening up of those in authority with the tactful presentation of gifts whenever necessary. On the contrary, Sir Arthur had the law tightened up in such matters. Even minor cases of official corruption were prosecuted with the utmost severity under his eagle eye. I had often perused his edicts on the subject, preserved in mildewed clothboard at the Government Archives. I had them much in mind on the opening day of the Sessions, since there was a long corruption case for trial.

Mr Manikswol, the auditor, was charged with numerous counts of fraudulent conversion. Having ample funds at his disposal, he had booked out the only hotel in the settlement, a whitewashed building like a Wild West saloon. I was obliged to move out to a small annexe at the rear. Unfortunately, we still had to share the same bathroom.

'Better be first in,' I decided, setting my alarm an hour earlier for the next day.

Dawn was breaking as I tiptoed past Mr Manikswol's bedroom door. His heavy snoring muffled my usual struggle with the kerosene water heater. It had to be a nifty tub because of leakage through a faulty plug fitting.

I was still sitting in two or three inches of tepid water when I suddenly realised that I was no longer alone. The snoring had ceased and somebody was gargling on the other side of the bamboo screen between bath and basin.

'Bathroom's engaged,' I called.

The suave face of Mr Manikswol, draped in the bathroom's only towel, appeared above the screen.

'Room for two, eh, Judge?' he sallied. With a curt nod, I snatched up my pyjamas and withdrew.

The following morning, I tried to reverse the batting order. For well over an hour I endured the cacophony of lungings, wallowings and other unimaginable bathroom athletics.

'All yours!' shouted the indefatigable Mr Manikswol, leaving a trail of puddles down the passageway. It was in fact the only trace of water left. An overhead clanking from the cistern and a smell of singeing in the heating apparatus told me there would be no bath for me that day. The bathroom, I decided reluctantly, would have to be avoided for the time being.

A body sponge was a poor substitute for a dip, in the heat of the tropics. The case dragged on for five sticky days. On the sixth morning, I proceeded with the summing up—Mr Manikswol having surrendered to bail.

The jury acquitted. The bathroom was free. As was Mr Gupla Deng Manikswol.

One last case remained in my list. A youth called Rami, the tearaway son of a local sugar cane farmer, was indicted for maliciously wounding a neighbour. It was the climax of a long-standing feud over land.

When I was leaving my hotel for court to hear this case, an envelope bearing the Government House crest was handed to me.

'Well, that settles it,' I told the Registrar, as I took my seat on the Bench. I had just opened the missive from Government House. It was an invitation to dinner again that night.

'We must finish this case today,' I announced.

'But the defence is calling twelve witnesses,' he pointed out. This was true. They were strewn across the court steps, fast asleep.

'Then the sooner we get started, the better,' I replied.

There was a ship leaving at dusk. With a bit of luck I could be on board by then, leaving behind a polite note to the Governor saying I was urgently required at my next port of call.

'Anything,' I decided, 'to avoid another night of disaster at His Excellency's festive board.'

The hot morning wore on. The prosecution closed its case.

'Your turn now, Rami,' I said to the accused. Rami, the Marlon Brando of the cane fields, wore a leather jacket and jeans. He opened his defence in a sort of Transatlantic accent, learned at the island cinema.

'Gen-l-men of the jury,' he drawled, 'I got myself an alibi. Guess where I was at the time this crime was committed?' The jury perked up. 'I was speedin' along the beach on a motor bike with my girl friend on the back.'

The girl friend, Rami's star witness, turned out to be a lady of generous proportions. She was equally generous with the truth. After cross-examination by the prosecution, she was obliged to admit with a smile that her story supporting Rami's alibi must be false.

'So everything you said was untrue?' I interjected.

'Not everything,' she answered happily. 'I give my true name.'

The girl friend was followed into the witness box by the eleven other defence witnesses, all relatives of the prisoner. I was somewhat preoccupied during the next hour recording their perjured evidence in longhand. It was the wheezing of witness number nine, the prisoner's cousin, which prompted me to look up. To my surprise the court-room was full of smoke. What plot was this? I wondered. A ruse to set the prisoner free? Or was the rival faction in the case taking the law into its own hands and planning to incinerate the prisoner, along with the Judge?

'Just the last stage in the cane cutting process,' explained the Registrar. Apparently, the farmer in the field adjoining the court-house was burning the stubble after harvesting the sugar cane.

'If Your Honour would care to adjourn,' he suggested, 'it will be all clear by tomorrow.'

'I can't do that,' I announced. The prospect of another evening with yowl and gung at Government House drove me on.

At long last the time arrived for me to sum up to the jury.

'Gentlemen,' I addressed them, raising my voice above the crackling of the fire, 'can you all hear me?'

'We can hear you, my lord,' called back the foreman, 'but we can't quite see you. Dusk was falling and the smoke in the court-room had rendered it very dim.

'You can take it I am still here,' I was able to reassure them.

The jury retired for twenty-five anxious minutes.

'Unanimous verdict of guilty,' announced their foreman, his head silhouetted against a skyline blackened with smoke.

Rami accepted his sentence in good part.

'Justice done there all right,' said the Registrar as I stepped out of court. 'If not quite seen to be done,' was my obvious reply.

I was still coughing slightly as we made our way past the smouldering cane field *en route* for the boat. 'Smoke no good for throat,' sympathised the Registrar. 'Better than His Excellency's mangrove liqueur,' I decided.

19

The Case Rests

My judicial buckle-shoes were not designed for a scramble over a coral reef. So it was hardly surprising that, when wading ashore at Koro Island, I came a nasty cropper in the process. I seemed to have cricked my back rather badly. 'Complete bed rest,' ordered the Island Medical Officer, a bluff Scotsman, as he dropped me off at the Circuit Judge's quarters. 'Justice will have to wait, laddie.' I had already decided otherwise. Laid up I might be, but work must go on. Dr McTaggart was reckoning without my knowledge of legal history. There was an obvious way out. I penned a swift note to the local Registrar of Sessions. 'Court to be held here in the Judge's Lodging,' I wrote. 'Usual time. 9 a.m.'

Lying under my mosquito net that night, I ran through the judicial precedents for my decision. In 1684 Judge Jeffries had summed up in the trial of Algernon Sidney 'Whilst being cupped and bled with a dozen leeches for the grype'. Chief Justice Kenyon conducted the Radnorshire Assize from his dwelling 'He suffered from the gout' (Payne's *Criminal Reports*, 1792, page 93). What was the odd lumbar twinge compared to these tribulations? I reflected. Nearer to my own times, at the Hilary Sessions of 1886, the then Judge's Lodging at Ipswich Manor House was used by Blair, J. for the Ryestone Burial Case. I munched dreamily on another large aspirin and floated off in an uneasy sleep.

Of course, in the light of a tropical dawn, the Judge's Lodging, Koro, was a bit different from the Manor House, Ipswich. It was a hut of woven palm fronds, at the far end of the village overlooking the lagoon. A bamboo verandah extended along the front.

'Prop me up on my charpoy and I'll be as right as a trivet,' I told the Registrar when he arrived. He was a slight, bespectacled man called Mr Lal. With the help of the houseboy, the ancient string-bed was brought out from the back of the hut. I was installed on it with my papers at my side. Pillows are not a Polynesian commodity. Mr Lal solved this by wedging a log-shaped native drum behind me, wrapped in a mat. After some discussion, the bedspread printed with pineapples was removed. Instead Mr Lal produced from his travelling bag a large Union Jack.

'Always handy,' he remarked, as he tucked it over my feet. I had to admit it lent some sort of formality to the proceedings.

'Call on the first case,' I said.

Koro was a trouble-free part of my circuit, and I did not expect a heavy list. A number of families were picnicking on the sand in front of me, awaiting the day's entertainment. Mr Lal had posted himself on a canvas stool on the verandah. 'One Billy Goat,' he announced, 'impounded under Section 47 of the Stray Animals Ordinance.'

The culprit was led forward at the end of a rope. 'Exhibit one,' said Mr Lal. Billy wanted to be friends. Slipping his noose, he joined me on the bed, where he slumped over my knees. He resisted all efforts to remove him. His BO was worse than his weight.

'Does the Section compel me to retain the creature,' I inquired through my handkerchief.

'Correct,' nodded the Registrar. 'Not to be released until receipt of poundage fee.' I directed a search for the owner.

'Without delay,' I stipulated.

Billy had already nibbled a corner of the Union Jack and was now browsing on my pyjama leg.

'How's the patient?' boomed a familiar voice. It was Dr McTaggart on his morning rounds. Billy stuck out a friendly hoof. 'It's the Judge's pulse I want to take,' the

Doctor told him. There was a round of applause as the Registrar translated this for the benefit of the audience.

'Strip off, then, Judge,' McTaggart ordered.

'Court adjourned,' I called. There was a hollow thud as I slipped back on my pillow.

'First yer blood pressure, if we can find any.' He started strapping my arm up in his machine. Billy thought it was some sort of game. It took a little time to release his horns from the rubber tubing. 'No infection's developed, anyway,' McTaggart announced. 'Should be up and about in a couple of days.'

There was no time for further examination. Mr Lal was already calling on the next case. 'Application for renewal of Licence—Wong Chai Cheng—Storekeeper,' he said. A small Chinaman was conducted towards the charpoy where Dr McTaggart was putting away his stethoscope out of Billy's reach. 'The Judge is the one without the beard,' he quipped as he stumped down the steps. Mr Wong nodded.

I was required to check his affidavit with the licence papers. There was also the usual 'swearing in' to be gone through. 'Chinese Oath?' I asked him. He nodded again. I beckoned to the Registrar. It was a ceremony I had witnessed elsewhere, but it never failed to impress with its air of exotic solemnity. Mr Lal had the necessary box of matches ready. He struck one of them and tossed it over his shoulder. 'If your application is containing falsehood,' he intoned to Mr Wong, 'may you be snuffed out like that flame.'

I had been writing for a few minutes before I noticed a peculiar smell in the air. 'You're not smoking opium, are you?' I demanded.

Mr Wong shook his head. 'Your Honour's bed is on fire,' he said.

Billy sprang across me. He caught my chin a graze before disappearing over the back of the verandah at high speed. Mr Lal took charge. He poured a clam-shell of water over me. Through the smoke Mr Wong was waiting for me to sign the certificate. 'Sorry about the smudges,' I coughed. I experimented with a nearby pandanus leaf as a blotter. 'The signature is completely valid, nonetheless.'

After a break for refreshment, the afternoon session went more smoothly.

'Last case,' announced Mr Lal. 'Obtaining by false pretences.'

'Who's the defendant?' I asked. A very old lady in long black draperies shuffled forward and squatted at the foot of the verandah steps. Fixing me with a beady eye, she drew a large circle in the sand. After a pause, she added a cross in the centre.

'This is Seru, the witch,' said the Registrar. 'She pretends to make dead people come to life again. All tricks.'

'No tricks,' said Seru, still busy with her noughts and crosses. 'I show Judge.'

There was, I recalled, an English case on the point. Mrs Duncan, the medium, faced a similar charge at the Old Bailey in the 1940s. The Recorder of London refused her request to invoke publicly the spirit world for the benefit of the court. But we overseas Judges were encouraged to be more flexible where indigenous tradition was involved.

'Very well,' I said. At least justice would be seen to be done, this time.

Chuckling to herself, Seru advanced towards me and began to fiddle with the shutter above my head. 'What are you doing, madam? I asked.

'Make darkness,' she explained. 'Spirit people not like sunshine.' All I remember is a loud splintering noise, a sharp pain across the back, then the darkness she promised.

'He's coming round,' were the next words I heard. I was looking up at the Doctor. 'Next case,' I said.

'Don't be ridiculous, man,' came McTaggart's voice.
'Where am I?'

'On the Medical Department launch on your way to the mainland hospital.' He fanned me with a large palm frond.

'A six-foot shutter landing on yerr back isn't what you need for a pulled ligament.' He exploded into a noisy guffaw. 'Lucky Seru didn't pack you off to the Spirit World!' The crew shared the jest, and elaborated on it all the way to our destination.

At least Chief Justice, Sir Neville Gawsby, took the whole affair more seriously. A few days later he flew in to see me.

'Bedside justice,' he exclaimed. 'Whatever next!' He cleared his throat. I handed him my glass of liver salts. 'And why on earth allow a demonstration of black magic?!'

'I was only following the Whitehall Directive,' I said. 'The one entitled "Bending the Law to Local Custom".'

'Well, no more bending, please,' said the CJ.

I pulled back the sheet and showed him the medical harness encasing me from the trunk downwards.

'Not much chance of that, sir,' I joked. The Chief Justice did not respond.

'Next morning, a bulky volume, smelling highly of insecticide, arrived for me. *The Pitfalls of Judicial Office Abroad*, read the title-page, by Sir Neville Gawsby, CJ. I somehow had the feeling I might have provided Sir Neville with an opening chapter for Volume Two.

Not that Sir Neville was the first person to advise me on the pitfalls of my office. That had been the privilege of Mrs Mungo Stubley, a fellow passenger on the SS *Mooltan*, the ship that took me to my earlier post in Arabia.

20

The Shadow of Mungo

'You can't spend the whole voyage on that bunk,' complained my cabin mate, a hearty tea-planter returning to Ceylon. 'Anyway, I've entered your name for the deck-quoits competition,' he added. 'Mixed foursomes. So you'll have to snap out of it.'

Our vessel had been pitching and rolling for five days—even my knuckles were turning green—but I put down Volume Nine of my travelling edition of Halsbury's *Laws of England* and tottered after him up to the sports deck.

My partner in the game was Mrs Stubley, a powerfully built lady with a very red face.

'I seem to be a long time finding my sea-legs,' I explained. I was a fool to draw attention to my legs. Even though my new drill shorts came down well over the knees, the absence of muscle in the calves, and the deathly white appearance, was startling.

'Try to concentrate on the game,' said my partner. I muffed another shot.

'You'll need a stronger arm than that,' said Mrs Stubley, 'if you're hoping to keep law and order in Arabia.'

It emerged that her late husband, Mungo Stubley, KC, had been a British Judicial Commissioner in the Middle East. Mungo Stubley had been something of a legend in his day.

'Here goes,' I said. I put everything I'd got into my last throw. The quoit flew right overboard.

'What a stupid way to lose us the game,' said Mrs

Stubley. She stalked back to her deckchair on the foredeck.

'Would you care for a drink, Mrs Stubley?' I asked. She put down her embroidery.

'You'll have to give that up for a start,' she said. I wiped my steaming brow. 'I was only thinking of half a shandy,' I said.

'Alcohol is strictly forbidden in decent Arab society,' said Mrs Stubley. 'Mungo considered it our duty to set the same example. 'The natives are always watching,' he used to say.'

She took a pack of chocolate biscuits from her Dubai travelling bag. 'If you're passing D Deck on your way down,' she said, 'you can drop these in for Basil.' I hadn't realised that Mrs Stubley's son was travelling with her.

'How old is the little chap?' I inquired.

'Basil is not little by any standards,' said Mrs Stubley. 'He's an Alsatian. And you'll find him in the Quarantine Kennels.'

I lost my way twice. They were helpful in the Boiler Room, but my reception in the Beauty Salon was very frosty. Ultimately the sound of barking led me to my destination.

'We've had to put him in a cage of his own,' said the Kennel Steward, when I asked for Mrs Mungo's pet. 'Unless you want to risk your hand you'd better leave these with me.'

I handed over the biscuits and hurried away.

Back in my cabin I returned to Halsbury's *Laws of England*. 'English law abroad,' I read, has a settling influence.'

The cabin ceiling was moving again. 'Could do with a settling influence,' I thought, overhearing my tortured stomach. 'Might as well see if I can get some lunch down.'

Luckily there was a stout mahogany rail right along the companion way to the dining-room.

'Ah, there you are,' called Mrs Stubley. She was towering over the cold buffet. 'It's bridge this afternoon,' she announced. I toyed uneasily with my bowl of consommé.

'Never quite got the hang of bridge,' I explained. Mrs Stubley snapped at a piece of celery.

'What about a round of Monopoly?' I suggested. Mrs Stubley winced. 'If an officer can't play bridge, he shouldn't be in the Service, was what Mungo always maintained,' she said.

Time, however, lay heavily on her hands, so the following afternoon she condescended to play. I had found a quiet spot amidships. The conservatory, they said, was directly above the stabilisers. Framed in Australian spider-lilies and a Mexican cactus, Mrs Stubley advised me about my future career, as I set out the board.

'You'll have to deal with a lot of feuding between Arabian tribes from time to time,' she observed, taking over the Chance cards which I had been trying to shuffle. 'That's when they may try to assassinate you.'

I gave the dice in my egg-cup a cowardly rattle.

'Blast,' I said, counting out my score, 'now I've landed in JAIL.'

'At least you'll be safe there,' commented Mrs Stubley, with something of a sneer, I thought.

I pulled myself together and was about to erect a cheap hotel in Islington when the bells rang for Lifeboat Drill.

We were both assigned to the same lifeboat. The Purser was in charge of our particular group.

'A couple of volunteers, please,' he called. Mrs Stubley was already there. She beckoned in my direction. I came out from behind the bulwark and the other passengers parted to let me through.

'You husband's looking a bit shaky on his pins,' said the Purser, 'but he'll do.'

Mrs Stubley decided to ignore this insult to the dead. With a grim smile she pushed me ahead of her into the lifeboat and then clambered aboard herself.

'Are you a good swimmer?' she inquired as the boat swayed on its davits down towards the water.

'Only at the shallow end,' I replied. It looked as though it might have to be the deep one this time, because the boat was now tipping dangerously to Mrs Stubley's side. I tried to hitch the lifebelt closer around me.

'Mungo was a swimming blue,' observed Mrs Stubley.

A jolt to the right of me made me open my eyes. The Purser had joined us.

'A bit of ballast needed on your side,' he laughed. To the cheers of the rest of the group we returned to the deck.

It was a relief to get back to the seclusion of the Monopoly table. I drew a card: 'PAY THE DOCTOR £50'.

'Not many doctors where you're going,' warned Mrs Stubley. 'Self-reliance was Mungo's motto.' She paused to check that I had paid out the correct money to the Bank. 'Know the answer to a scorpion's bite, for instance?' she asked.

'I don't think the question came up in the Bar Finals,' I chaffed.

'Mrs Stubley advanced sternly to GO.

'It would soon wipe that smile off your face if you suffered one,' she reprimanded. I took my next turn, only to land on the Water Works already owned by my opponent.

'Water,' said Mrs Stubley. 'Always in short supply in Arabia.' She took a bonus from the Community Chest. 'Mungo could go without a drop of water for two days provided he was wearing a pith helmet.'

I sipped at my lemonade. Perhaps I should have heeded what the Manager at the Tropical Outfitters in London had advised, I reflected.

'If you're going to live in Arabia,' he had warned me, 'you'll certainly need a sun helmet.' He disappeared up a shop step-ladder.

'The Kipling,' he called, toppling a large white dome from its cobwebbed sanctuary. He trapped it firmly under one arm and descended with care. 'The finest in pith helmets,' he said, 'steel-lined and fully ventilated.'

I crunched it into position.

'Does it always come so low over the eyes?' I demanded of a tailor's dummy alongside. 'Try pulling it down at the back,' suggested a sales assistant.

'Must be the wrong size,' I complained. The Manager came to my assistance.

'We don't want to be a figure of fun before the Bedouin, do we, sir?' he reproved, swivelling the helmet the right way round.

'I prefer to do without it altogether,' I had told him.

'It's your move, you know,' barked Mrs Stubley, interrupting my reverie.

I hastily turned my attention back to the game. 'Here goes,' I called, trying hard for a double six. My score was two. 'I seem to be on Park Lane,' I said. Mrs Stubley held out her hand.

'Which means you owe £1,200 rent,' she declared. That was the end of the match.

We had bright weather across the rest of the Mediterranean, but I maintained a dim record at our daily Monopoly sessions.

'I'll be leaving you here,' announced Mrs Stubley when our ship docked at Port Said. Apparently she now lived in a bungalow at Alexandria.

I felt duty bound to escort her ashore. Basil came with us.

'Mrs Stubley,' I called down the gangway. 'I don't think Basil wants to be friends.' His nostrils were already distended.

'He doesn't like your rolled umbrella,' laughed Mrs Stubley, calling the brute to heel. 'Mungo always carried a sword-stick.'

It was heavy going along the wharf with one of Mrs Stubley's portmanteaux in each hand. 'The porters here demand such outrageous tips,' she complained.

She pointed towards the customers' car park behind Simon Artz, the famous tourist gift-store.

'I parked my little runabout in there,' she said.

I was surprised to find her Austin 7 still intact. Even in Egypt, it seemed, nobody dared steal from Mrs Stubley.

She and Basil forced their way inside, along with the portmanteaux.

'The battery's flat,' said Mrs Stubley. This was hardly surprising since she had been away in England for three months.

'Give me a push from the back,' she ordered. She and Basil watched my futile efforts to get the vehicle in motion.

'Mungo could have lifted a car this size,' said Mrs Stubley.

At last the engine jerked into life. She and Basil poked their heads through the window. I made my farewell.

'Not a patch on Mungo,' I heard one them murmur, as they drove away.

I was subsequently to discover that Mrs Stubley was not untypical of those formidable memsahibs who played an important role in the British Raj. It was not, however, until the late nineteen fifties that I visited the South Sea island of Wagatoka. There I first heard about the most remarkable of all the Daughters of Empire.

21

Lady B

In the great roll-call of imperial pioneers—Kitchener of Khartoum, Chinese Gordon, Lord Milner, the Marquess of Curzon—the name of Bertha, Lady Frampton has, I have discovered, been overlooked. This is surprising. For while General Kitchener was making imperceptible progress towards the capture of Khartoum, and long before a plan for representative government in the Transvaal occurred to Lord Milner, Lady Frampton had established her famous Imperial Temperance Movement.

My researches show that she and her husband, Sir Horace Frampton, an elderly baronet from Wiltshire, spent ten exhausting years documenting 'the prevalence of alcoholism in the British Colonies'.

Following the publication of their findings, Lady Frampton addressed a packed meeting of temperance supporters in Sussex Hall, Cheapside.

'Australia,' she reported, 'is demoralised by gold-fever with strong drink the chief agent of ruin.' Sir Horace lumbered among the audience, distributing copies of his wife's latest tract, *Morning Dew Drops*, extolling the virtues of water.

'From Australia we returned to Cape Town,' Lady Frampton proceeded, as Horace set up the magic lantern. What looked like a huge whale appeared on the screen behind the speaker.

'There we found one drink-shop for every hundred inhabitants,' she explained. Sir Horace was struggling to insert his slide of Table Mountain the right way up.

'Arriving back in New Zealand,' the speaker persisted,

'we were confronted by a scene of similar depravity. The aboriginals of that country, a race unsurpassed for physical vigour, formerly knew only water. Their happy ignorance has, alas, been dispelled, so drunkenness is widespread. But their chiefs did not hide from us their contempt for the white missionaries and their addiction to rum—*kakina te waperu*, "stinking water" as they call it.'

'Shame,' applauded the Vicar of Cheapside from the front row.

'The assembly dispersed after a bumper collection for Lady Frampton's Movement. Increasingly busy though she became with organisation, Bertha Frampton still found time for theological research. She was convinced that the wine used at the Last Supper was non-alcoholic. Clad in a large beaver hat, she searched the Mediterranean countries for 'the true biblical wine'. Eventually, she tracked it down in a Benedictine monastery on the island of Sardinia.

Upon receipt of her exciting news, Sir Horace joined her. Together they sampled what turned out to be 'boiled down grape-juice'. It was, using Lady Frampton's words, 'a sugary liquid of rosy hue', which gave Sir Horace a fatal attack of renal colic. He survived long enough to read the draft of his wife's latest article for the *Canadian Theological Gazette*.

In this, Bertha tackled Paul's advice to Timothy: 'Drink no longer water but use a little wine for thy stomach's sake and thine other infirmities.' 'The Saint,' she declared, 'was referring to the very beverage of which my husband and I have now partaken.'

'Yes, of course,' agreed Sir Horace, closing his eyes with a sigh of relief. He left his widow comfortably endowed.

However, much later in life, she contracted a second marriage to Walter, the harmonium player at her Sussex Hall rallies.

'We shall be leaving for the Cannibal Isles,' she informed him, four weeks after the wedding ceremony. It was— according to the Frampton Papers, kindly placed at my disposal by her great grand-daughter—the morning of Lady Bertha's sixtieth birthday.

'The baronet and I docked there on our way back from New Zealand,' Bertha noted in her Day Book. 'I sent Horace ashore on his own. He confirmed my worst fears. The scenes of alcoholism were the worst in the whole of the Empire.'

Later that day, she addressed the Southwark Band of Hope—according to a cutting from the *Teetotal Progressionist*. 'I've felt a call to the South Seas ever since,' she told the enthusiastic meeting.

It was then that Walter learned, for the first time apparently, that his wife had already booked their passages out there.

'I'm a lucky man,' he had written to his sister, when Lady Bertha proposed to him. He was not, perhaps, quite so sure about this when they were boarding their steamer at Tilbury in the teeth of a North Sea gale. Nevertheless, they had the very best cabin from which, the Log suggests, Walter did not emerge until the ship reached the calmer waters of the Pacific. Then he took up a perch, like a sparrow, at the foot of Bertha's chaise-longue on deck.

'Bertha cannot abide intemperance,' he explained to the Captain, 'particularly among the cannibals.' Captain Langford nodded approvingly. Lady Bertha, voluminous in her silks, reminded him of his days under sail.

At last, on Easter Sunday, they anchored off Underlau, the capital of the Cannibal Isles. Captain Langford needed no compass to guide him into the harbour. He merely followed the line of empty gin-bottles floating out from Underlau on the evening tide.

The little port was a rowdy settlement of beachcombers and naval deserters.

The visitors stayed with Edgar Bayard, the British Consul, who happened to be a distant relative of Sir Horace Frampton.

'Great Uncle Horace was fond of a good claret, according

to family tradition,' said their host, his hand on the decanter at the dinner-table.

'Not once he was married to me,' snapped Lady Bertha.

To the astonishment of the Consulate staff, she removed the stopper and discharged the contents into a vase of hibiscus flowers. All conversation rapidly petered out.

The principal bedroom, where Lady Bertha retired with an overnight glass of Epsom salts, adjoined Underlau's principal hotel, the Melanesia. The noise from under its tin roof grew more riotous by the hour.

'Now you can hear for yourself how sorely they need temperance here,' said Bertha, throwing back the mosquito net. Walter, his little pink ears flattened between the pillows, smiled wistfully.

'Poor ignorant natives,' she sighed, 'poisoning their systems with alcohol.' She was not to know that the natives were excluded from the hotel.

The islanders had other ways of poisoning their systems. Only recently they had cooked the Reverend Joseph Barker, Baptist minister on Cacadelevito, in his wellingtons, and downed him, boots and all.

'The worst alcoholism is on Wagatoka in the outer islands,' lied Edgar Bayard at dinner the following night. He could think of no island in the group more distant from Underlau, and after twenty-four hours of barley water, Her Britannic Majesty's Representative was desperate.

Three weeks later, Lady Bertha and Walter arrived on the American brig *Charles Doggett* at the island of Wagatoka. Lady Bertha, bone-corseted in the prow, supervised the unloading of Walter's harmonium into the long boat. The Chief of Wagatoka, Saafu, forewarned of their visit, awaited them on the shore. Lady Bertha viewed him through her opera glasses.

'A slovenly, nasty looking fellow,' she commented. What Saafu thought of Lady Bertha is not recorded, but he had learnt from the fate of his cousin that it was wise to affect hospitality towards white visitors.

His cousin, Chief Naradodoa, head of the neighbouring island, had believed himself invulnerable to gun-shot. A blackbirding party from the *Stanley*, a Queensland slaving ship, found the Chief unwilling to trade his people for calico and washing blue. Fighting broke out, during which the Chief strutted defiantly in an exposed place. A rifle shot killed him before he could appreciate his mistake. His death, however, was revenged by the people of Wagatoka who ambushed the slave-dealers on Wagatoka Sands. Their captain and two companions took refuge on a high rock. At dusk, the captain decided to go down to negotiate a truce. He was promptly seized and plunged head-down in the water, roasted, and his more edible portions distributed among the tribal leaders. The other comrades managed to escape during the night.

'I wish to make it quite clear,' Lady Bertha announced to Saafu,' that I have not come here to be eaten.' Saafu looked hurt. 'And as for my husband,' she added witheringly, 'you can see for yourself what a poor dish he would make.'

Walter was paddling ashore, his trousers rolled to the knee. 'I intend to open a Cocoa and Reading Room on the island,' she explained to Saafu, later on, through an astounded interpreter. 'My mission here is to wean you away from the foul intoxicants to which I know you are at present addicted.'

They enjoyed a pleasant overnight-stay under a palm-leaf canopy specially erected for them.

Next morning, Saafu arranged for a formal presentation of *yagona*, a custom learnt during the days of Fijian occupation. *Yagona* is made from the dried root of a shrub. It is mixed in a large four-legged wooden bowl, the *tanoa*. This is placed at some distance from the presiding chief, with its plaited cord and white cowrie shells laid out towards him. When the *yagona* is ready, the cord is wound up, the cup-bearer moves forward, his cup filled. He turns to face the chief. Holding the cup with his arms fully extended, he sinks to his knees, every muscle taut. He then fills the

chief's cup from his own. The chief drinks and, amid hand-
clapping, he spins the cup back to the mat. When Lady
Bertha was presented with the *yagona*, she assumed that it
was alcoholic, and instantly threw it away. Apart from the
fact that it was not, of course, alcoholic, her action was an
unforgivable insult. Saafu said nothing at the time. It
happened that a site had been prepared in the village for
the erection that day of a new *bure* (house) for him.

The building was to be 78 feet long and ten feet high. Its
centre post, already hewn to shape and polished, was four
feet in circumference. The woven bamboo for the walls had
been collected. So had the reeds for the thatched roof.

Before construction could begin, however, a living
person had to be buried upright, clasping the great central
post for the ridge pole. But it had to be a person of imposing
physique and dominant personality. Only then would the
mana or mystical power of the chief be strengthened.

Saafu inspected, with satisfaction, Lady Bertha's massive
biceps; then remembered his duties as a host. 'Our little
white man,' he decreed, 'will accompany the village
children to the beach.'

The ceremony was carried out in Walter's absence. The
words of the accompanying chant, 'the lowering of the
post', are still remembered in the South Seas.

During the weeks that followed, the new widower sat
quietly by the lagoon watching the breakers curl on the
reef. 'I like it here,' he decided. Fortunately Saafu had
become fond of him.

In those days it was fashionable among the leading
chieftains of the islands to boast a tame white man
amongst the entourage, particularly one who played the
harmonium. Walter remained on Wagatoka for many
years, before retiring to Tasmania.

He was allowed two. wives, whom he selected with
meticulous care.

According to the Wagatokans, Lady Bertha, once having
passed over, acknowledged her mistake. She approved of

yagona-drinking. So much so that the *yagona* ceremonies held in the new *bure*, over which her indomitable spirit presided, were always occasions of good omen. Until the Wagatoka Chief took to whisky-drinking in his old age. A particularly drunken orgy seems to have proved the final straw. 'Quite enough,' Lady Bertha reputedly decided, and let go the centre post. The post crashed down, killing the Chief and two of his companions.

However legendary this last part of the saga, Lady Bertha's influence definitely lived on in the Liquor Prohibition Laws which I was required to enforce. Consumption of alcohol on the islands was strictly controlled by a permit system.

The Wagatokan elders, who aroused my initial interest in Lady Bertha, agreed to take me to the site of the chiefly *bure*. It lay on the edge of the main village. The thatch had collapsed and the site was a mass of creeper.

'The centre post is still where it fell,' I was told. 'It has never been moved.'

I was keen to see underneath. If there was any truth in the final episode, I should find there a pile of bones and the shattered fragments of a whisky bottle.

Unfortunately the fallen post was piled high with sacred stones. 'May I dig around a bit?' I asked.

'Very sorry,' explained the interpreter, 'there is a strict taboo on the shrine. Nobody is allowed to approach within three arms' length.' So ended my field study of this intrepid Lady of the Raj. Legend and superstition took over where historical inquiry left off.

22

Law and Order

On the Bench, as everywhere else, two heads are sometimes better than one. Especially in strange surroundings. So, at many of the settlements on my circuit, I developed the practice of inviting the local Stipendiary to sit with me wherever feasible. It worked very well. The only exception proved to be Noumoa, when Hoskyn Boggis held that particular job.

Years of isolation seemed to me to have given Boggers, as he was usually called, a cavalier approach to the status of judicial office. He apparently saw nothing odd in asking me, when I arrived, whether a friend of his could join us on the Bench.

'Didn't know there was another European on the island,' I said.

'He's of local descent,' Boggers replied.

Of course, one wants to do everything one can to encourage local people to take an interest in affairs. 'But,' I had to point out, 'my circuit trials aren't exactly social occasions.'

There were also the provisions of the Criminal Procedure Code to be taken into account. 'Is he, for example, a qualified lawyer?' I asked.

Boggers led the way towards the court-house, an army surplus nissan-hut. 'I think you'll find, Judge,' he said, 'my friend Henry has all the qualifications required.'

A devoted procession of tiny children followed the Stipendiary Justice down the path between the hibiscus bushes. One carried his whisky bottle. Another his banana sandwiches for tiffin. A third had his special barkcloth cushion. The last one carried his rolled umbrella.

We took our places at the little bamboo table facing the public area, and I began the usual pronouncement for opening proceedings.

'Oyez, Oyez, Oyez,' I declared. I was startled to hear a fourth 'Oyez' croaked out on my right.

'Leave it to me,' I murmured. I hoped Boggers wasn't trying to take over my role.

'All manner of men draw nigh,' I went on, 'and give your attendance at this *court*.'

'Cawk, cawk,' rang out just behind me.

I turned my head to encounter a large green parrot sitting on the back of my chair.

'This is my friend Henry,' said Boggers. He dug into his pocket and offered Henry a handful of peanuts.

'You'll find him indispensable,' he added, 'I always do.'

'That's your affair,' I snapped, 'but I'm not having my court made a mock of by a wretched bird.' As I spoke, I felt a sharp tweak on my right earlobe.

'Henry's very sensitive, he can pick up the slightest change of tone,' warned Boggers.

I decided it was best to ignore this farcical situation. I shifted forward in my seat.

'Will the defendant in the first case step into the dock, please,' I said, and indicated the small compartment of plaited rushes. There was a buzz of interest at the back of the court.

'Order,' I called.

'Awker,' said Henry, hopping onto our table.

'Knows it all,' murmured Boggers, 'like the back of his—er—claw.'

'Perhaps just one of you could stop interrupting,' I complained. 'I am *trying* to concentrate on the work in hand.'

The defendant, a chubby young man in a flowered sarong, was charged with joy-riding on the Post Office Bicycle.

'How do you plead?' I asked him.

'Not Guilty,' he answered.

'Nark Gilkey,' echoed Henry. His black eye was severe.

The spectators nodded approvingly. Unlike me, they seemed to take Henry's presence for granted. A volley of peanut shells was discharged in my direction as Henry attacked his lunch.

'Enough is enough,' I exploded. 'He must be removed.'

'I'm afraid you don't understand,' Boggers persisted. 'The parrot is venerated in these parts. Look at those old ladies over there. They're looking at him as if he were the Archbishop of Canterbury.' This, strangely enough, was true.

'Their Ancestral Deity is the Parrot God. So what Henry says is law. Isn't it, Henry?' He patted the bird on the head.

The parrot had begun to scratch through my case papers. I signalled to the court usher.

'Bring my travelling set of Halsbury's *Laws of England*,' I requested.

Upon my instructions, the usher stacked all the volumes between myself and Henry. For the time being at least I was sheltered from the creature. Apart from an occasional twitter, Henry remained thankfully quiet while the case proceeded. The evidence was overwhelming. The defendant was undoubtedly the youngster who had been seen with the Official Push-bike. The moment arrived for the verdict. I summed up and announced that I found the charge proved.

'Mr Boggis,' I said to the learned Stipendiary, following Section 18 of the Criminal Procedure Code, 'what is your opinion?'

'Not Guilty,' declared Boggers.

'Nark Gilkey,' agreed Henry, choosing that moment to perch on top of the *Laws of England*.

'That's two to one, old boy,' said Boggers.

'Mr Stipendiary,' I whispered, 'do you seriously think I can accept a parrot as a member of the Bench?' I was quite determined. 'He must be removed from court,' I said, 'however sacred he may be.'

'Well, I'm not taking him,' said Boggers, 'and you'll never get anyone else to do it.'

I was anxious to avoid an untoward scuffle, single-handed with the brute, especially if, as I feared, Henry emerged the victor. Then where would British Justice be? An adjournment was the only solution.

'Would you kindly retire with me?' I said to Boggers. I stood up and bowed to the assembly. 'Alone,' I added, with what I hoped was a meaningful glance at the parrot. We withdrew to the seclusion of the nearest ivi tree.

'Come, come, Mr Stipendiary,' I said. 'You know perfectly well the correct verdict is guilty.'

Boggers hitched up his baggy drill-shorts. 'True,' he said, 'but the defendant's basically a decent lad. Know his family well. A shame to have him start out with a criminal conviction to his name. Besides, I need him to take me out fishing tomorrow.'

'He is a first offender,' I responded, 'and for that reason—and no other—I'm prepared to give him a conditional discharge. That doesn't count as a conviction, as you know.'

The Stipendiary stroked his beaky nose; in profile he bore an irritating resemblance to his wretched friend.

'Done,' he agreed.

We returned to the court. From his seat on the law books Henry had kept order during our absence. The audience waited in silence. We took our seats and I turned formally to Boggers.

'What is your opinion, Mr Hoskyn Boggis?' I repeated.

'Guilty,' he declared.

'Gilkey,' confirmed Henry.

I discharged the defendant with a warning. The decision satisfied everybody, especially Henry. He accepted with lordly aplomb a mixed tribute from the reverent populace—mostly green mangoes and melon rind.

It was, I supposed peevishly, in its ludicrous way, a scene comparable to the mediaeval tradition of patron saints associated with English Law. One had to be flexible about such things, I told myself. As Halsbury comments, 'It is in the pomp of the Assize Court that the vigour and power of the ideal of justice is really brought home to us . . . One gets a sense of a great engine of justice, powerful and all seeing, of checks and counterchecks which it is impossible to evade . . .' Certainly Henry had qualified for the last clause.

Next morning Boggers was down at the quay to bid me farewell. Henry was on his shoulder, still keeping an eye on things The inter-island schooner was waiting for me off the reef.

'While I am Resident Stipendiary,' Boggers said, with a smile, 'there's one thing you will always have on this island.'

'What's that?' I asked, as my launch edged away from its moorings.

'Law,' he called, *'and Order.'*

'Awkar. Awkar,' came Henry's voice following me across the lagoon.

I returned to Fulala in a mild state of shock. 'What on earth do you make of it all?' I asked my neighbour, Ursula St Alban. She had joined me on the front verandah, where I was calming my nerves with an extra sundowner or two.

'Did you know that Hoskyn Boggis has a great reputation as a practical joker?' the headmistress inquired.

I gulped down my double vodka. Now that she mentioned it, I began to recall an amused glint in Boggers' eye!

'Everybody knows he's been teaching that parrot to perform for years,' she added.

I angrily swotted a sandfly. 'A court of law is the very last place for childish tomfoolery of that sort,' I complained.

Miss St Alban observed me archly. 'Hoskyn Boggis

wouldn't be the only judge with a bit of schoolboy in him, would he?'

I decided to reserve judgement on the subject and changed the conversation.

23

Incidents in an Outpost

It was not until the following March that another memorable episode disturbed my routine. I was working in the Law Library on Overlei, at the time. Just as I was replacing a book on the shelf, I felt the ground move under my feet.

'Must be an earth tremor,' I decided. They were common enough throughout Polynesia. Then it happened again.

I edged my chair away from the shelves. I certainly did not want Jowitt's *Dictionary of Words and Phrases* on my head, quite apart from the *Encyclopaedia of Legal Forms and Precedents*, Volumes 1 to 6. The next moment I felt a hand grasp my ankle. I looked down to discover a gaping split in the floorboards. Through it, I recognised the balding dome and scarlet features of Professor Hans Koch.

The distinguished archaeologist had been conducting a survey of Overlei for some time.

'You shouldn't be excavating here,' I said. 'It's Government Property.'

'At least you can give me the helping hand,' enjoined the intruding academic.

'Certainly,' I agreed, 'if you release my foot.'

I was naturally annoyed, for the library had only recently been completed. In fact I myself had initiated its construction. At each of my regular courts on the circuit, there was need for a library of up-to-date commentaries on current law. Unfortunately, because of lack of space on Overlei, that one had had to be squeezed in between the courthouse and the adjoining village cemetery. Even so, I was proud of this modest brain-child of mine, with its neat roof of dried cow-dung and shelves of banana crates.

Dr Koch levered himself up to safety. Breathing heavily, he sank into the nearest chair and began to polish his tropicalised bifocals with a red silk handkerchief. 'I am examining the tomb of King Lika,' he explained,' when, zoomph! I make breakthrough!'

The grave of the famous island King was marked by a huge coral plinth, the side of which had made a handy fourth wall for my new library. Until now, I had not wholly appreciated that the burial vault itself ran right under the library floor.

'I'd like to see your documents of accreditation for this particular dig,' I insisted.

As I spoke another floorboard gave way.

'Take care!' called the Professor. A small mountain slide had begun over at the General shelf. Gatley on *Defamation*, Rayden on *Divorce* and Chitty on *Contract* (14th edition with supplement) disappeared in a cloud of dust. It was clear that the matter could not be resolved there and then. I retrieved my notes in the case I was working on—a tricky point in the sequestration claim against the Breadfruit Workers' Union—and made for the door.

'We'll resume this discussion first thing tomorrow, Dr Koch,' I said. 'Please come and see me in court.'

The following day, I was surprised to find an angry crowd had assembled on the court-house verandah. There was a loud hissing as I went through and took my usual seat at the Judge's Table. Unfortunately, it seemed that the usual village trouble-makers had put it about that I was somehow to blame for what had happened. The Lika Mausoleum was regarded as sacrosanct. Now it had been desecrated and the Royal Spirit itself disturbed. Who knew what vengeance might be wreaked upon Overlei! Professor Koch was already sitting at the table opposite me.

'By rights, Professor,' I began, 'the ball's in your court, not mine.'

'What is this about balls?' he complained. 'Here is my papers. All correct.' With a flourish, he pushed across a bundle of documents. 'My honour is without stain,' he insisted.

'That's more than can be said of my jacket,' I pointed out, retrieving an overturned inkwell. I was dabbing at the magenta spots on my lapel when a ripe mango caught me in the eye.

'Constable Timothi!' I called. 'Kindly keep the crowd in order.'

I moved away from the window and continued my scrutiny of Dr Koch's credentials. He was apparently relying upon a General Permit to Remove Artefacts granted by the Home Office under Section 18 of the South Pacific (Archaeological Expeditions) Order in Council 1933.

'That's all very well,' I said, 'but I'm still not happy with this particular excavation. After all, you can see I'm the one who's getting the brunt of it.' The sound of drumming floated in from the village square. 'I must see for myself precisely what you propose to do.'

'Very well, we go now,' agreed Dr Koch.

Outside, the constable was brandishing his truncheon at the nearest agitators. With a noisy mob at our heels, we made our way round to the cemetery.

The entrance to King Lika's tomb was sheltered by a huge ivi tree and many of the protesters had climbed into its branches.

'Tell them I'm simply making an inspection to see that nothing has been disturbed,' I said to the constable. I followed the Professor down into the burial chamber. The air was dank and some of the steps had crumbled under a thick growth of Samoan strangle-weed. The Professor's torch flashed ahead of me in the darkness.

'What was that?' I exclaimed.

Something had caught in my hair, or rather in my wig. It was only a tomb-bat, but I was rather on edge. Suddenly the Professor shone the light on the stone sarcophagus. To my relief it looked as if it were still intact.

'You see,' he called, directing his torch to the base, 'these are what I wish to remove.' Along the plinth lay a variety of pottery artefacts.

'Excellent examples of the Polynesian pre-Christian culture,' his voice echoed. 'All will be safe in my custody.'

'Out of the question,' I said. 'The people would never agree to their leaving the island. It would provoke a total breakdown in public order.'

'But I must insist,' the Professor began. 'I have permit.'

I mopped my brow with the edge of my tippet. There were sounds of increased agitation outside. Rapid thinking was needed.

'Will you agree to leave it to me?' I said.

The Professor nodded dubiously.

'It might take some time,' I warned him. 'These people can be rather determined.'

A huge crowd blocked every side when we returned to the entrance. Some of the men had put on war paint and were jumping up and down in what was obviously a preliminary battle dance.

'Interesting how these folk-rituals have survived the impact of the western civilisation,' the Professor remarked, as I sidestepped an ethnic throwing-club. At any moment a stern reading of the Riot Act might become necessary. Fortunately, Constable Timothi managed to hustle us to safety through a side exit.

Excitement gradually died down, although it took me a whole week of patient negotiations with the tribal elders to persuade them to meet the Professor half-way. The artefacts could be brought out—but they must remain on Overlei. Some kind of permanent exhibition was the obvious solution. As Professor Koch remarked, there was only one place for it.

So it was that the Koch Museum and Law Library was opened to popular acclaim. Sir Neville Gawsby formally approved the arrangement.

'An excellent illustration of the Equitable Principle of Fair Compromise,' he wrote.

In the museum section, the prize exhibit was a gigantic earthenware cooking pot. Once used by King Lika for cannibalistic purposes, the gruesome utensil was unique in being designed as a double receptacle. Sitting at my studies, I sometimes reflected how comfortably Dr Koch and I would have fitted into it, had things gone another way.

There had been a time when things would indeed have gone another way. In 1832, Commodore John Bryan (Foul Weather Jack), after calling at Overlei and the nearby Savage Isles, commented: 'The inhabitants of these parts are proverbial for their cruel and barbaric habits. From what we ourselves have witnessed, they are rightly named Savage Peoples.'

Some fifty years later, however, the Superintendent of Christian Missions in the same part of the South Seas was able to report: 'Our toil in these heathen lands has borne great fruit. The eating of human flesh has become extinct. Polygamy is fast dying away. Infanticide is declining. With the coming of the British Flag, human life is no longer reckoned cheap. The avenger of blood comes not as a stealthy assassin or backed by savage warriors, but invested with the Solemn Dignity of established law.'

24

The Best of Both Worlds

Solemn dignity seemed to have deserted me when I myself flew the short trip from Overlei to the Savage Isles, 600 miles east of Tonga. I was sitting up front with Captain Ashley Patterson, the Australian pilot. The only other cargo was a package of hymn-sheets for the Savage Islands Brass Band.

Suddenly the plane stalled violently, throwing me into the Captain's lap. We had run into an electric storm.

'Why do Judges always have to break the law?' he complained. I had unlocked my seat-belt, contrary to regulations.

There was a clap of thunder and a vivid flash bounced off the right wing.

'You'd better grab a hymn-sheet, sport,' he added, as he wrestled with the controls. 'Make it "Abide With Me"!'

Fortunately, Captain Patterson was a brilliant aviator. He put the plane back on course, and soon afterwards took it down safely on to the landing-strip. Once there, he helped me good humouredly to unstrap my trunk of law books from under the rear petrol tank.

'Perhaps I brought you a spot of luck this time,' I said, pointing to a battery of small holes in the side of the trunk where the lightning had struck.

A smiling customs official waved us past his bamboo enclosure, trimmed with a hedge of hibiscus.

I took my leave of Ashley Patterson.

'Good on yer!' he said, with a farewell punch in the chest. He walked back towards his plane. 'Wotch out they don't swipe yer wig-box,' he called. 'Queen Emma might fancy it to keep her tucker in.'

As the aircraft taxied away for take-off, a Landrover drew up beside me. 'Alloa,' welcomed the driver, a dazzling young man in a mandarin-style tunic with blue and gold epaulettes. Kalawi was the name by which he introduced himself. He was the nephew and secretary of Queen Emma, reigning Sovereign of the Savage Islands Protectorate.

'We have to go straight to the Palace,' he explained. I pointed out that the journey had been rugged in the extreme. I was in dire need of a barber and hadn't seen a shower bath for several days.

'I'm afraid Her Majesty is very infirm,' Kalawi told me. 'On doctor's orders she can only manage an audience this afternoon, before returning to her country retreat for a long convalescence.'

We drove at a sedate speed through the island capital of weatherboard stores and thatched houses, then to the Palace gardens. As we passed through the open gates, Kalawi turned on the wireless. 'Here now is Billy Haley playing "Rock Around The Clock", as requested by the Station Sergeant and the Boys of Police Headquarters.' To the sound of Haley's Comets we drew up at the main verandah of the Royal Residence. A palace guard came down the wide flight of steps and opened the door for me.

Kalawi conducted me into the Palace. It had the tranquil air of an English rectory at the turn of the century. There were antimacassars and photographs of various royal personages, including King Edward VII and George V.

'Her Majesty Queen Emma,' announced her nephew.

The Queen, a grandmotherly lady in a Chinese dressing-gown, was propped up on a dais of finely embroidered mats. She fingered a string of blue prayer-shells. About her the walls were hung with Victorian prints of biblical scenes—gifts from the missionaries, no doubt—*The Return of the Dove to the Ark, Ruth in the Gleaning* and *Abraham with Isaac*.

I made my salutation in front of *The Disciples* by J. Arbuthnot, ARA, a canvas of enormous size.

I badly needed a change of clothing and a haircut, while

my three-day growth of stubble was particularly disfiguring.

'An interesting likeness,' said the Queen, pointing to Mr Arbuthnot's representation of Judas Iscariot, immediately to my right. I tried to change the subject.

'A significant honour for me, ma'am,' I began, 'to serve as your visiting Judge.'

'It's of great importance to us, too,' said the Queen. 'You're the sixth in line of succession, you know. May I ask your denomination?'

'Middle Temple,' I replied. The Queen cleared her throat. 'I was referring to your religious convictions.'

'Oh, C of E,' I blushed. The Queen looked relieved.

'I thought you might be an unbeliever like so many white men these days. And that would be the one bar to your appointment.' She handed me a Royal Parchment and a pen. I clocked in under the Royal Cipher and the ceremony was over.

Outside, Kalawi was waiting to take me to the Judge's Lodging, a gloomy edifice erected in 1890 with imported terra cotta for Justice Charles St Stephen.

'I'm so sorry you caught my aunt on one of her off-days,' were Kalawi's final words as he left me to settle in.

For the next hour or so I worked steadily at the marble washstand in the vast uncurtained bedroom.

'Better put the rest of my clothes away,' I decided, fairly satisfied with my respectable new image in the mahogany standing mirror. The chest of drawers was lined with the yellowing pages of the 'Empire Stores Shopping List, Pall Mall, 1911.' My clean handkerchiefs went on to the sheet advertising 'Twilfit Rustproof Corsetry for Memsahibs Everywhere', while my pyjamas covered the descriptions of 'Wilkinson's Mixture—Pronounced by the Highest Authorities as the Most Wonderful Purifier of the Human Blood and the Safest and Most Reliable Remedy for Torpid Livers in Hot Climates', 'Huxley's Ner-Vigor Tonic for All in Imperial Service who feel Unable to Work through Enervation and Nervous Debility' and 'The Blue

Nile Ointment for Severe Inflamed Conditions of the Skin, Dhobi-itch and Other Equatorial Eruptions'.

A polite knock on the bedroom door interrupted my reading.

'Arta-noon tea ready, sah,' called a man's voice. I went out to be greeted by Samuela, the cook, a white-haired Savage Islander with several broken teeth. He had laid out tea beside a long-sleever cane chair in the dining-room.

'You do this job for long time?' I inquired.

'For life, sah,' he beamed. I stirred the sugar into my tea.

'You must really like the work, then,' I observed thoughtfully, 'to want to stay here for ever.' Samuela looked puzzled.

'I get life, sah,' he said.

He pointed through the open window. At the bottom of the magnolia garden a wicket gate swung open in the ocean breeze. There was a rusty board on it. 'HM Gaol', it read.

Samuela passed me a plate of hot buttered scones.

'Are you a prisoner, then?' I asked. He nodded. 'The only one,' he boasted.

I took a puzzled bite of the scone.

'You've certainly cooked this very nicely,' I approved. 'What was your crime?'

'I kill my daddy,' he replied. 'Give bad food. No pain. He go down dead very quick.'

I spent an uneasy post-prandial half hour until Kalawi arrived with the case files for court next day.

'He's perfectly safe,' he reassured me. 'It's not a habit of his. It was his father's land he was after.' He paused politely while my stomach rumbled. 'Let me know if you'd like a royal food-taster, though. We have one we could spare.'

I laughed it off and turned to the files. 'Poisoning of livestock' met my eye. 'At least they've moved on to the animals,' I reassured myself.

Most of the cases were appeals from decisions of the local magistrate. All pretty straightforward, I thought, as I made my way next morning into the Second Drawing-Room of the Judge's Lodging, which constituted my court-house.

Kalawi helped me out as *amicus curiae*, but it proved a tiring day. By late afternoon, we had dealt with one action for breach of promise, two boundary disputes and three nuisances on the public highway. The light was failing as I turned to the final matter on the Case List. Kalawi recited the facts.

'Volo ordered a dugout canoe from Jaki and gave him five dollars for it. Jaki did not make the canoe because Hovolu took three dollars from him. Hovolu did this because he had supplied his father Soru with a stick of tobacco, part of which was given to Dini, Volo's father. Dini did give Soru two dollars for the tobacco and also for some turtle he had supplied. Soru still did not pay Hovolu, but spent the two dollars. Soru has now promised to borrow a dollar to give Hovolu and Hovolu has paid three dollars to Volo and promised to make him a canoe. When the canoe is finished, Volo is to pay over three dollars. The magistrate has ordered that the two dollars are to be handed over within two months and the canoe completed within three months.'

The Prince resumed his seat behind a spray of ferns.

'Something of a tangle,' I said wearily. 'Who exactly has appealed?'

'Everybody,' replied Kalawi.

He bent a kindly ear in my direction. 'It may not be quite as difficult to resolve as you think,' he said. I wondered why. 'I understand,' continued Kalawi, 'that none of the appellants is still alive. Rather an old case I'm afraid.'

Time, I discovered, had its own special meaning in the Savage Isles. This brought my opening Session to an end.

'There's just the criminal trial for tomorrow,' said Kalawi. 'Case of shopbreaking.' It was all that remained for me to deal with on that particular visit.

'I'll leave you to study the prosecution evidence,' he said.

Prince Kalawi's command of English was not surprising, since he had been educated abroad. But the overall high standard I had met in the island capital was due to the

Mission teaching. This was where the island magistrate had been schooled. He had recorded the statements of the prosecution witnesses with copperplate precision.

The accused, it seemed, had been seen leaving the shop in the early hours of the morning, with a large carton of Coca-Cola balanced on his head and a dozen pairs of Aertex Y-fronts—two products of the West which had most impressed him. Three by-standers had intervened to deprive him of his loot, but failed in the struggle. The one flaw in the case was that none of these witnesses had been asked by the police to identify the accused on a parade.

When I joined Kalawi in the Court Drawing-Room, next morning, the first thing he did was to pull on the bell rope. 'A little refreshment before we swear in the jury and start the case,' he said.

I pushed an open volume of Halsbury towards him. 'I'm afraid we can't start the case at all,' I replied, waving away the tray of orange drinks. 'Your police don't seem to have heard of the law on Identification Parades!'

I read from the relevant paragraph in Volume 22: 'The defendant selects his position among eight men of similar appearance to himself and the witnesses are each given the opportunity to pick out the accused.'

Kalawi handed me a glass from the salver. 'Identification of this defendant may not be the problem you imagine,' he suggested.

'Out of the question,' I said. 'English criminal law is littered with cases of mistaken identification—from Oscar Slater onwards. Matter of principle.'

At that moment the defendant appeared in the doorway to surrender to his bail. His face was tattooed with stripes of red and green. He wore a large boar's tusk through his nose.

'He's the hereditary high priest from the last of our heathen islands,' explained Prince Kalawi. 'Fell into crime on a visit to the capital.'

'Does he always look like this?' I asked faintly.

'He's no alternative,' said Kalawi. 'Goes with the job. It's all done at his consecration.'

Not unexpectedly, the jury convicted before midday.

I ordered the defendant to join the cook in the garden penitentiary where I paid a last visit with Kalawi before leaving for the airport. The shop-breaker stood cheerfully to attention to greet us. He had a half-empty bottle of Coca-Cola in his hand and was clad simply in crisp new Aertex Y-fronts.

'The quality of mercy is not strained in these islands,' said Prince Kalawi. 'The shopkeeper let him keep a couple of samples of his haul.'

'Christian charity,' I approved.

'And a heathen prayer for increased profits in return,' rejoined Kalawi with a final handshake. 'It's the best of both worlds in the Savage Isles.'

I rather agreed with Prince Kalawi. The islanders, I noticed, always threw frangipani blossom into the sea (the traditional offering to the Whale Deity, Nouranja) on their way home from church.

Their church had been founded by Missionary Arthur Tombs. 'We give thanks to Our Redeemer for Edith's sewing machine,' the Reverend Tombs noted in his diary of 1891. 'By means of this Modern Marvel, my wife, dearest Edith, has furnished Cotton Smocks for each of the young womenfolk here. Their near-naked bodies are now *decently* concealed, God be praised.'

A minute to Arthur Tombs from the Savage Islands' first Medical Officer took a different view. 'Tropical rains are heavy,' Dr R.H. Reeves pointed out. 'On bare skin the water dries quickly and naturally. These sodden English garments you have led them to wear merely cause respiratory troubles.'

Doctor Reeves failed to convince anyone of the unsuitability of Western dress for the South Seas. I lost the same kind of argument over my Judge's Regalia, and sartorial problems continued to plague me.

25

Boggers Again

The trouble had really begun back in London—the day I went to get myself kitted up at Ede and Ravenscroft, Judicial Outfitters, in Chancery Lane. All went well until we got down to the long black stockings. The assistant disappeared and there was a whispered conference outside the fitting room curtains. Mr Jossling, the manager, took over.

'I understand we're a bit short of muscle, my lord,' he said. He bent down and gave my calf an investigative tweak. The stockings concertina-ed another inch.

'For the garters to hold up, sir . . .' Mr Jossling coughed. 'May I make a suggestion, your lordship?' He glanced over his shoulder. 'A, er, lady's suspender belt sometimes does the trick.'

This was easier said than done. I was leaving the very next day. I telephoned my Aunt Sylvia at her Red Cross Overseas Office in Pimlico.

'It's hardly the kind of thing we supply,' she replied, 'unless you want a surgical support!'

When she had stopped laughing at my expense, I obtained her directions to the lingerie department at Marshall and Snellgrove. 'Ask for the mature matron's model,' she added.

The stout no-nonsense affair, produced after some confusion behind the counter, stood me in excellent stead for a number of years. Until there came a crucial moment half-way through the Assize Service in Fahiti . . .

I was reluctant to go to Fahiti in the first place. For the new Resident Judge there was none other than Hoskyn Boggis of parrot fame, or rather ill-fame!

However, Boggers had made a point of calling on me in Fulala, before taking up this new appointment. He had stood me a bibulous dinner at the club, where I had been persuaded to see the funny side of the parrot episode.

'Had to part with Henry in the end,' Boggers had laughed, over our final brandies. 'Blighter was getting above himself!'

The letter that Boggers had now written to me from Fahiti seemed to be on the level.

'Can you please help out at the Fahiti Assizes?' he wanted to know. He went on to explain that he would be tied up with a long case of fraud involving the Fahiti Minister of Agriculture and a shipment of rotten bananas to New Zealand. 'Could you handle the other cases?' he inquired. I decided to let bygones be bygones and flew over to join him.

I arrived just in time to change into my regalia for the traditional church service the day before. Hoskyn Boggis, also robed, awaited me at the steps of St Winifred's Anglican Mission of the Assumption—a corrugated iron building overlooking the mangrove swamp. A guard of Honour was lined on either side.

I fell in smartly behind Boggers, as ten warriors closed in to form an archway of crossed warclubs.

There was a bit of a hitch in the doorway. The Paramount Chief, wearing the ceremonial headdress of Noumoan Tamarisk, greeted me with a bow, trapping my shoulder-sash in one of his lower branches. The church-warden came to the rescue and I soon caught up with Hoskyn Boggis. Together we processed up the aisle over a carpet of Polynesian barkcloth.

'Watch your strep, old chap,' whispered Boggers. He had obviously primed himself for the occasion. There was a ripple of amused chatter from the congregation, seated cross-legged on mats. 'You're not in Westminster Abbey, y'know.' Inquisitive fingers tugged at my gown as I picked my way through.

'Quite so,' I agreed.

We sat down in the solitary Official Pew at the front, with Boggers taking up more than his fair share of space. Pandanus leaves and fruit had been used to decorate the seating arrangement. I began to move a large clump of pineapples from my end.

'Taboo,' hissed Boggers. He considered himself an authority on ethnic custom in that part of Melanesia. In fact I had only recently received a copy of his latest paper on 'The Decline of Ritual Sneezing in Melanesian Culture'. (*Transactions of the Oceania Society*, Volume 74, 9-73).

'The sacred fruits of the land—sort of harvest festival,' Boggers went on to explain. He stretched across me and carefully restored the pineapples into position.

'Let us pray,' interjected the deep voice of the Reverend Josua Popo, officiating minister and honorary assize chaplain.

'We give thanks for the presence here today of Justice Knox Mawer, and of our own Mr Hoskyn Boggis. Let us not forget that they are known to us as the *Salima Vulavi*—the Root of the Law. We beg that they may long time prosper and flourish among us.'

'Amen,' agreed the congregation. Apart from the back row, a section reserved for juvenile delinquents from the local Approved School.

As befitted a formal occasion, the service was delivered in English. Boggers, on the other hand, preferred to display his command of local 'pidgin'. Especially with the hymn singing.

'Big Boss Boy savvy me in heaven,' he boomed in a deafening baritone. Mrs Popo, at the organ, peeped out anxiously through the curtains, then speeded up the pace. We got through the seven verses in under two minutes, long before the collection had finished. I placed my sixpence into the clam-shell, held out by the churchwarden. Hoskyn Boggis dropped in what looked like the lower half of his dentures.

'Sharks' teeth,' he explained, 'the traditional local currency.'

It was time for the anthem, an excerpt from Bach's B Minor Mass performed by the village schoolmaster on the Tahitian Nose Flute.

'A dying art,' Boggers explained. At that point I myself might have closed my eyes for a few minutes, had I not been all too aware of the activities of the Judge's Beadle. Armed with his ornate staff of office, he was prodding awake the drowsy. The 'Readings' lasted even longer than the anthem.

It must have been the prolonged kneeling on the bamboo foot-stool that put the final pressure on Aunt Sylvia's equipment. Whatever the cause, I felt something vital give way.

'Gird up thy loins, thou Hypocrite,' were the next words I caught from the Reverend Popo. That was exactly what I was trying to do.

'And get ye hence from the House of the Lord.' Willingly, I said to myself. But it was a difficult thing to do with one's stockings at half mast, and trailing a lady's suspender belt.

Under cover of the pineapples, however, I embarked on a daring new ploy. I managed to remove the stockings altogether, and slipped them into my tropical wigbag.

Just as I was about to put my shoes on again, Boggers glanced towards me.

'Good thinking,' he said. To my astonishment, he began to follow suit.

'It's local custom to go without shoes on consecrated ground,' he announced, 'so why not us?' Once again, I seemed to be involved with Hoskyn Boggis in setting a curious legal precedent.

Boggers had kept on his sunglasses throughout the Assize Service. So I never did know whether there was another twinkle in his roguish eye.

26

The Rehabilitation of Young Offenders

Odd though it seems, juvenile delinquency was a problem even in the South Seas. What was I doing, inquired Chief Justice Gawsby, in a searching minute on the subject, to try and keep these youngsters out of the courts? I decided to consult Major Smythe, over a drink at the club.

Major Reggie Smythe, MC, was devoting a vigorous retirement in the islands to Voluntary Work.

'Youngsters drifting into the capital away from traditional village disciplines—unemployment—getting into trouble with the law—increase in juvenile delinquency,' I outlined the problem to him. 'I've persuaded the Roman Catholic Mission to let me have the use of the Church Hall for these lads,' I explained. 'Trouble is, I haven't had much response so far from the young people themselves.'

The Major stirred the swizzle-stick in his pink gin.

'That's where you come in,' I said.

'Leave it to me,' he replied.

Major Smythe was as good as his word. 'Look in on us,' he said, two weeks later.

Down at the Church Hall I came upon tremendous activity. All of it had been organised by the Major. Boxing was going on in one crowded corner. There was table tennis in another. The towering figure of the Major himself was outside, conducting a First Aid class. My arrival caused a painful lull in proceedings.

'You see my problem,' I confided to him. 'I'm keen to help, but when many of these lads last saw me, they were in the dock and I was handing out their sentences from the Bench.'

The Major was shaping a heap of palm fronds into bandages.

'Is there any way I can regain their confidence?'

Major Smythe put away his penknife.

'Very easy,' he barked, 'Just fall from that acacia tree and break your leg.'

I blinked.

'Only pretend, for heaven's sake! I want you to be a patient for the boys to practise their first aid on.'

I was dubious.

'Participation,' he stressed, 'that's the secret of success with the Young.'

I began to grasp the way his mind was moving.

'It's vital in your case,' he said. 'Let them see you joining in. That way they'll begin to accept that the law has a human side.'

Major Smythe is right, I thought.

'Just shin up a few feet, then fall back,' he said. 'Make it as vivid as possible.'

I was not prepared to go that far.

'I'll just spreadeagle myself at the foot of the tree,' I agreed.

A buzz of excitement greeted this unexpected exhibition on my part.

'Our first job, lads,' said the Major, outlining the object of the exercise to his team, 'is to locate the injury suffered by the Judge.'

He bent down over me. 'You're supposed to have broken your leg below the right knee,' he said.

I made a show of pain in that direction.

'To find the fracture, boys,' Major Smythe continued, 'we have to compare the injured limb with its sound neighbour.'

Suddenly, and quite without permission, he sliced off both my trouser legs with his penknife.

'It's sheer vandalism, Major,' I complained. What especially irritated me was that they were my only pair of formal trousers. It might not have been so bad had he cut the legs less jaggedly, or at least to an equal length.

'Perhaps nobody will notice anything's wrong if you wear your gown on top,' said Major Smythe, 'but by all means charge any damage to my mess account at the club.'

The First Aid class of delinquents was now helpless with laughter. It took the Major a few minutes to restore order.

'Let's assume the break is here,' he said. Using a dampened guava stick he tattooed a cross under my knee cap. 'Next we look around for splints.'

One of the class ran down to the shore and returned with a pair of canoe paddles.

'A bit on the large side,' said Major Smythe, 'but they're certainly strong enough.' Under his supervision, one paddle was placed under me and the other on top.

'Pull on the injured leg below the fracture,' he instructed, 'then bind fast the splints.'

There was no shortage of volunteers for this operation.

'For goodness sake,' I protested, 'tell them they're not supposed to be weight-lifting now.' I suppose the youths themselves were not conscious of their strength.

'How does that feel?' the Major inquired.

It was not so much the weight of the splints that concerned me as their disproportionate size.

'I'm very boxed in,' I said. It was almost as though I was in a three-quarter-length coffin.

'Place your left forearm across the chest,' he said, 'with the palm towards the body and thumb upwards.'

'What good is that going to do?' I wondered.

He placed my elbow in the middle of a broad coconut frond. 'We're assuming you've also broken your collar bone,' he explained.

I remained gloomily silent while eager brown hands encircled my upper body with a tight girdle of pampas grass.

'Final exercise,' he announced. 'Stretcher-bearing!'

It transpired that the First Aid class had already made a

litter for this purpose, using branches of rain-tree bound with sinnet.

'Lift the patient on to the stretcher,' Major Smythe directed. Shielding his eyes from the sun, he pointed to the headland which rose steeply behind the Mission compound. The Cable and Wireless Station lay on the top.

'For the purpose of this exercise,' he said, 'the Cable and Wireless Station is our nearest Medical Post.'

A narrow path led through the bush behind the Catholic Mission and followed the contours of the headland up to the Telecommunications Building.

'We'll have a bit of a competition,' the Major directed. 'One relay team will carry the Judge up the path. The other will bring him back.'

He called on the first two runners. 'Josefa and Samueli,' he said by way of introduction. 'Athletic fellers, both of 'em.'

I knew both candidates well. They had recently been paroled, after a period of detention give by me for causing grievous bodily harm.

'Keep the litter steady,' said the Major as we set off.

My carriers negotiated the first stage of the journey well enough.

'Speed it up,' called Major Smythe from below. He was timing us with a stop-watch.

The next two members of the Outward Team were poised at the take-over mark. This was at a point where the track turned sharply above the northern slope.

'Don't forget the Judge has to go back to his court before long,' called the Major. 'We don't want any increase in crime while he's away.' This was perhaps true, although I would not myself have mentioned it at that particular moment.

'OK, Boss,' grinned Samueli. He said something in Fulalan to Josefa and they broke into a sprint towards the take-over junction.

I am almost sure that what followed was due to over-keenness on their part. I did feel that Josefa was rather showing off when he disengaged his right hand in order to snatch a yellow thornflower and place it jauntily behind his ear. But I have no evidence at all that they were deliberately not taking proper care of me.

As we swerved into the bend I could, of course, feel that I was at an angle. And I rather think I called out a warning—'Remember, lads, I've nothing to hold on to'— just before the final catastrophe. Certainly I might have been better prepared for it had my view of things not been hopelessly restricted by my foliage of bandaging.

From the excited voices of the waiting pair of runners there is little doubt as to the ultimate cause of disaster— they tried to pass me over without the slightest reduction in speed. Whether or not somebody stumbled so that the stretcher completely overturned 'on the snatch', as it were, I cannot say. What I do remember is the final plunge down the bank into a bush of wild lime.

'No harm done,' I assured the Major, as his stretcher-bearers hurried to my assistance. He was full of apologies.

'Are you sure you're all right?' he asked.

'Perfectly,' I replied.

I removed the last thorn, before making my farewells.

'For one moment you seemed about to give the class a chance to practise *real* first-aid!' he said. He began to chuckle.

"'Participation" has its limits, Major Smythe,' I told him coldly, 'even where I'm concerned.'

27

Olympics in Paradise

After the war, as everybody knows, the World Olympics went through one crisis after another. However, a crisis was something I had not expected where the South Pacific Games were concerned.

It happened on Tavoni, a principal island in the eastern quarter of my jurisdiction.

There was an unfortunate confrontation between me and the Provincial Commissioner on the verandah of the PC's House.

'It's hard luck,' said the Commissioner, 'but your court-house will have to be demolished.' He cleared his throat. 'Er . . . removed in some way, that is—otherwise the Games may have to go to Fiji.'

Great pride was felt that Tavoni had been selected as the site for the next Island Games. I was on the Organising Committee and the first meeting was in progress. Like everyone else, I was full of enthusiasm for the project, until the PC's opening remark struck me like a blow.

'But why the court-house, Commissioner?' I asked. 'Surely there's space elsewhere?'

'You know our problem as well as the rest of us,' he said.

It was by now very hot, with the sun overhead on the corrugated iron roof—the time of day when tempers became frayed.

He pointed through the palm trees beyond the verandah. The steep hillside and overhanging cliffs rose up within a quarter of a mile from the shoreline. The thatched village houses and the trading centre were clustered thickly in every available flat space between the lagoon at one end of the island, and the jetty at the other.

'You do see yours is the only possible site for any kind of Sports Arena,' the PC went on.

All eyes turned to my court-house a hundred yards away, a wooden structure dating from early Colonial days. The green sward which surrounded it was one of its chief attractions, setting off the quaintness of the fretwork surrounding the miniature portico.

'It's an historic building, Commissioner,' I insisted. 'Listed under the Pacific Conservation Trust.'

'Historic!' snorted Chivers, the Information Officer. Chivers had never forgiven me for the £2 fine for keeping an unlicensed dog, a savage little bull-terrier.

Stung into action I enlarged on the theme.

'It's where the Council of Chiefs appointed the first British Judge in 1887. It's where Captain Palmer, the notorious slaver, was brought to justice. The Court Proceedings were referred to in the House of Commons by Disraeli himself.'

The Secretary for Sport and Physical Education threw back his head and roared with laughter.

'Just look at the place,' he said. 'Talk about demolition! It only needs a couple of front-row forwards to put the boot in and the job's done.'

I glared at him with hatred. Were all Rugger Blues such philistine oafs?

'It happens to be made of seasoned weatherboard,' I retorted. 'The only example of Cottage Rococo in the South Seas.'

'Now, now,' interrupted the Committee Treasurer, Canon Horton, polishing his glasses. 'No point in getting steamed up. I'm sure everything can be settled in an amicable spirit.'

'Yes it can,' ruled the PC. It was five minutes past his midday gin. 'A vote, gentlemen, please. Those in favour?'

A forest of hands went up around the table. He didn't bother to ask for those against.

'I'm sure you'll find alternative accommodation,' he said. He dropped a heavy hand on my shoulder. 'After all,' he smiled, 'you're as much entitled to justice as the next man.'

So I was, I resolved. When roused, no one can accuse me of procrastination. My appeal against the decision went off by the next diplomatic bag.

Other legal problems took over as I proceeded on the circuit—the case of the Namba Tapioca Biscuit Works versus the Queen, for instance, and the Bigamy Trial of Pastor Olaf Christiansen of the Church of Latter-Day Saints. I put the court-house matter out of my mind until I was back in Tavoni again. There had been no reply to my communication and I made a mental note to check next day on the progress of my objections.

Meanwhile the backlog of cases that had accumulated in my absence had to be dealt with as usual. I found myself appreciating the old-world charm of the court-house more than ever. I brushed away an industrious squad of termites from the ledge of the desk and removed the lei of hibiscus flowers someone had suspended over my old mahogany seat and hung it over my wig-box.

'Appellant Samuel Nako,' called the Prosecuting Inspector. 'Charged with theft, sir. Arsony of a fishing net.'

'The word is larceny,' I observed.

'That is what I said, Your Honour.'

I sighed. 'How do people expect me to hear properly with all this banging on the roof?'

It was the time of year for the replacement of the hurricane supports. Surely they could have waited until the Sessions were over, I thought. I'd have a sharp word for Saunders, the Government Engineer, when I saw him in the club over the weekend.

'The next appeal is wrongly dated,' said the Inspector— he sidestepped neatly to avoid a fall of plaster—'as Your Honour can see.'

'That's precisely what I can't do, at the moment,' I

replied. A particle of mortar had lodged itself in my right eye.

I was probing under the eyelid with a corner of my handkerchief when a sheet of corrugated iron crashed to the floor. Fortunately the canopy bearing the royal coat of arms had preserved me from a direct hit.

'What are they doing up there?' I demanded blindly.

'Removing Your Honour's roof,' the Inspector replied.

'Roof?' I echoed through the dust.

'Commissioner's orders,' the Inspector continued.

As my vision cleared I made out a face grinning down through the open rafters. There was something oddly familiar about it, something I associated with Criminal Records.

'Isn't that Isikeli the pig robber?' I exclaimed.

The face nodded delightedly.

'Prison labour is being used for the demolition work,' the Inspector explained, prising away the iron sheet from between me and my desk.

He straightened himself and produced from his pocket a letter stamped with the Provincial Commissioner's seal. I ripped it open without ceremony.

'My Dear Judge, sorry not to give you more notice,' the PC had written. 'An official delegation from the Pacific Games is coming to inspect the site next week, so our plans have had to be accelerated, I'm afraid. Apologies for the inconvenience but people are breathing down my neck, and you know how that feels.'

At that moment I certainly did. Somebody large was standing directly behind my shoulder. I turned and found myself confronted by Harish Moka-moka—Big Hari as he was known on the island. I noticed he was carrying a sledge-hammer. We hadn't met since I gave him five years for robbery with violence at the last Sessions.

I drew myself back. A deep breath usually helped in that kind of situation.

'I wish it to be publicly known,' I announced to the

excited crowd now dispersing in all directions, 'that neither Mr Moka-moka nor anybody else has my permission to continue this work of vandalism.' My words were drowned in the sudden roar of an internal combustion engine outside.

A cheer went up. Isikeli was at the controls of the Public Works bulldozer—*Ni-Sa-Manda*, or She-Who-Devours, as it was locally known.

'Hadn't we better adjourn?' shouted the Inspector in my ear.

I nodded.

'All manner of men having anything to do before this Honourable Court may now depart,' the Inspector began somewhat unnecessarily, I thought. 'God Save the Queen.'

I bowed and took a step backwards as the Inspector wound up the formal peroration. 'And God Save the Judge.'

On this occasion He didn't. Moka-moka had removed the steps leading up to the Bench and I came to rest under a pile of Bastardy Applications.

I picked myself up and made for the doorway. Moka-moka was standing guard, smiling broadly, apparently indifferent to the effects of his thoughtless action. He presented arms with his sledge-hammer as I limped past him and made my way to the Judge's official motor, a black six-cylinder Austin of pre-war design.

The Inspector was busy removing the film of dust from the bodywork with a couple of banana leaves. He was not quite in time, however, to prevent my seeing the slogans scrawled across the bonnet.

'GAMES OK,' it said on one side, and 'JUDGE GO HOM' on the other.

A group of youths, glistening with body-oil, rolled with helpless laughter under the mango tree.

'That settles it,' I declared. I jumped into the driving seat and engaged the clutch with a savage jolt. 'I am going straight to the Provincial Commissioner.'

My interview with the PC was painfully abrupt. All attempts at reason on my part were useless. A fortnight later the Supreme Court of the islands was reduced to a small marquee on the beach.

As it happened, the opening of the resumed Sessions clashed with the first day of the Games. I wished we were not in quite such close proximity—less than a hundred yards between my tent and the other running-tracks.

For the sake of good will I put up with the noisy throngs, the constant interruptions of competitors trooping to the sea for a dip, and the pineapple-and-peanut sellers pitched outside the open doorway.

In the minds of the visiting islanders, the court and the Games were all part of the same festivities. In fact, whenever the running events palled, spectators would crush together onto the trestle-benches to watch the case in progress—sometimes joining in with cries of encouragement.

'This is a court of law,' I warned, from my shaky platform erected at the top of a ladder, 'not a Sporting Occasion.' This merely produced another outburst of enthusiasm.

I did wonder if things had gone too far when I found my robing-room—a tiny wig-wam at the back—invaded by a team of weight-lifters from New Caledonia, practising with their dumb-bells.

I kept my patience, however, and on the final day of the Games my restraint was rewarded in a somewhat unusual way.

The presentation of medals had been going on during most of the morning and the applause for the last of the victors had died away. Suddenly my court proceedings were interrupted by a delegation of Games officials in traditional mat-skirts and garlands.

'They are wishing to address Your Honour,' announced the Inspector.

'Come forward, gentlemen,' I replied.

Their leader smiled.

'One more award to make, sir,' he said.

He held out a large coconut-shell. In it was set that rarest of Pacific shells, the Golden Cowrie. There was an inscription around the base.

'A Gold for the Judge,' it read, 'Umpire of Justice.'

28

Strains and Tensions

Fond though I had been of the court-house at Tavoni, it was of modest proportions.

'So this is the cricket pavilion?' a visitor to the island had once inquired. I expected him to know better. A judge's knee-breeches and hose are not generally mistaken for batting-pads and cricket boots. But tourists in that part of Oceania often behaved as in some sort of dream. This was perhaps understandable. When I paid my first visit there, I myself felt slightly unreal. On my inaugural day, a troupe of hula-girls performed a highly suggestive dance of welcome; while Mr Rama, the Court Registrar, wore a red hibiscus flower behind his ear.

'Just two cases of coconut embezzlement,' he announced. Everybody was smiling, including the defendants.

'We pay our fines in bananas,' they explained, with a bow.

After three weeks of banana trifle for tiffin, I consulted the Provincial Commissioner about an amendment to the law. The words 'or other fruit' were added to the Penalty Section of the Criminal Procedure Code.

The staging of the South Pacific Games in Tavoni seemed to bring changes. Somehow life became less carefree afterwards. Not that the forensic scene had been free of tension. Upon one of my earliest visits, for instance, a particularly acrimonious case came before me. It involved family rights of inheritance to the estate of the late Mr Pacifica Noa. The main item of property was the family outrigger, made from a hollowed-out tree trunk. This was dragged into court complete with its traditional six-foot oar of elaborately carved teak.

'Exhibit one,' noted the Registrar.

Mrs Mathilda Noa, the widow, claimed sole possession. 'Everything for me,' she insisted.

As Captain Cook recorded in his log of 1776, 'Ye womenfolks of the isles be mightie stronge.'

Mathilda was no exception. There was no question of squeezing her into the witness-box. Instead we cleared the front row, where she settled down, spreading her flowered silk dress majestically around her.

The deceased's brother, Sairusi, a wizened farmer in a straw *sulu*, disputed Mathilda's claim.

'She no good wife,' he wheezed. 'Always make big trouble. Husband only small small fellow, like me.'

Mrs Noa snorted contemptuously.

'She like too much toddy,' Sairusi added. 'Always drunk.'

At this point Mathilda lost patience. Rippling her biceps, she picked up the heavy oar like a matchstick and took a broad swing at her brother-in-law. The little man ducked out of danger. The dignity of office did not permit me to move so swiftly. Fortunately I was caught merely a glancing blow on the shoulder. Otherwise I should undoubtedly have considered committing her for contempt.

'Do right without fear or favour, prejudice or ill-will'—the words of my judicial oath are always at the back of my mind.

'Judgement for Mrs Noa,' I pronounced.

Right must be done according to the law, not according to the passing discomfitures of the Judge. Even so, it was quite in order to issue a stern warning.

'From now onwards, madam, I suggest you mind your Ps and Qs,' I said. Although my advice may have lost something in translation, the implication was clear enough.

However, the stresses of that sort of judicial maelstrom were very much the exception. Generally speaking, things were calm and predictable. Which is why I was taken by surprise during the conference with the Tavonian Director of Public Works. He somewhat resembled Mrs Noa in build, except that he was about a foot taller.

The subject under discussion was the rebuilding of my seat of justice. 'For the time being, Judge,' said the Director, 'you must use the Temple of Paradise.'

I must admit I was bowled over by this one. The Temple was simply a ruin. It dated from pagan times and was now largely inhabited by bats.

'I don't think there are any toilet facilities, Director,' I demurred.

He fingered his necklace of sharks' teeth. 'Some arrangement can be made,' he promised, 'if only a temporary one.'

It was like holding court in Stonehenge. A gigantic circle of coral pillars surrounded a grass enclosure kept in trim by the sacred Temple Sheep. The Registrar had rigged up a fairly comfortable Bench of barkcloth on what had probably been the sacrificial altar.

'What happens when it rains?' I asked Mr Rama.

'We adjourn, my lord,' he replied.

This was all very well, but neither of us had thought of the prevailing trade wind.

'*Now* what do you suggest?' I exploded on the following afternoon. We were half-way through the first case when a sudden gust whipped off my wig, carrying it right across the lagoon, where it disappeared into the blue.

'Not to worry, lordship,' Mr Rama answered.

I was extremely worried. Under Section 6 of the Court Regalia (Overseas Territories) Regulations judges were not allowed to exercise jurisdiction bareheaded. The case I was trying, a flagrant breach of the Tidal Warnings Ordinance, had attracted a throng of villagers to my open-air tribunal. They were now agog with excitement at this unexpected drama.

'Come back tomorrow,' the Registrar told everybody.

I spent a restless night in my bungalow. I was pensively toying with my toasted breadfruit next morning, when Mr

Rama arrived. Under his arm he carried a mysterious
bundle wrapped in pandanus leaves.

'My wife,' said the Registrar, untying his parcel with a
flourish, 'Champion of Handicraft at the Women's Institute.'

I could hardly believe my eyes. The ingenious lady had
fashioned nothing less than a replacement wig. I examined
the framework of bamboo, around which she had skilfully
woven several hanks of white wool.

'Where on earth . . . ?' I began.

Mr Rama beamed.

'Temple Sheep, my lord. Bring good luck maybe.'

Together we lowered it into position. Under the circumstances it was not at all a bad fit.

So, in full regalia again, I took my place in the Austin 6,
which doubled as a hearse when not in judicial use. The
Registrar had gone on ahead and I soon joined him for the
resumed sitting of the Tidal Warnings Case.

'Evidence from the Coastguard, please,' I directed.

All went smoothly during the early part of the officer's
testimony. Then I became aware of a new and sinister
development.

We had, of course, no court barometer, only a large piece
of seaweed. Glancing at it, I noticed beads of moisture on
the leaves, the tell-tale sign of abnormal humidity. I raised
my hand and encountered the worst. The bamboo latticework had begun to warp. In next to no time a cascade of
white fluff was falling over my spectacles.

At first, I was able to exercise a measure of control by
discreet insertions of blotting paper. However the situation
soon became hopeless. With a loud crack the main strut
gave way and clamped itself firmly over my ears.

'You must excuse me,' I told the Coastguard. 'I can no
longer hear the evidence.'

At that moment I noticed the Registrar making efforts to
attract my attention. I freed my left ear, feeling rather like
a disc-jockey in a pair of headphones.

'What is it, Mr Rama?' I asked.

'It's Tavanga the fisherman,' he said. 'He says he has something special for your lordship.'

I shook my head—an involuntary movement which I instantly regretted. It toppled the entire makeshift edifice to the ground, where it slowly disintegrated.

There was a ripple of applause from the spectators.

'Tell Tavanga,' I said, 'my cook has already bought some goats' kidneys for my supper, so I'll not be buying fish today.'

Tavanga proved strangely persistent. He forced his way right up to the Bench, his catch in a net over his shoulder.

'How many times?' I expostulated. 'Nothing at all wanted today.'

With bold insistence, Tavanga thrust his catch towards me, a repulsive grey object still dripping from the sea.

'And I certainly don't want octopus,' I snapped. 'He knows I dislike the stuff. Especially after the last time.'

Three empty bottles of Dr Collis Brown's Convulsion Mixture, by my bedside, were a silent reminder of that unhappy episode.

'Not octopus, my lord,' Tavanga insisted. He dug into his net and waved the catch before my eyes. With some difficulty I recognised the soggy coils of my missing wig.

'Lordship's Magic Hair,' smiled Tavanga.

Within minutes I was over in Mr Rama's office, using his radio-telephone.

'Sir Neville Gawsby, please,' I told the operator at the Pacific Commission Headquarters in Sofoa.

'What is it?' demanded the surprised voice of my chief.

'I can't put up with these humiliations a moment longer, CJ,' I burst out.

'I appreciate you're upset,' said Sir Neville, 'but there's no need to scream at me.'

I hastily adjusted the knob marked 'Atmospheric Distortion'.

'You simply must exempt me from wearing this idiotic

regalia, sir,' I went on. 'One item or the other brings me
nothing but trouble.'

'I shall write to you on the subject,' were the Chief
Justice's final words.

His letter proved a sharp disappointment.

'As you know,' he wrote, 'the Court Regalia (Overseas
Territories) Regulations are binding on us all. They were
framed by Bubbles Starkey (Lord Axmaster), the former
Government Legal Adviser, whose fag I happened to be at
school. Let me quote his explanatory words: "Even in the
remotest corners of our Empire, it is the visible presence of
the red judge, in traditional attire, which reassures the
righteous and deters the evil-doer."

'My own views could not be better expressed,' Sir Neville
concluded.

So there the matter rested. The following week saw me,
in my dried-out wig and customary scarlet, dutifully
struggling ashore at Vomo, the next port of call on that
Assize.

29

The Crisis Deepens

'Do I have a heavy list for trial?' I enquired of the Prosecuting Inspector, who greeted me at the entrance to the Meeting House overlooking the lagoon. This constituted a court of law for my visit to Vomo Island.

'Just one case of careless driving,' he replied.

'But surely there are no cars on Vomo!' I said.

'Correct, lordship.'

Puzzled, I adjusted my steaming robes and straightened the tippet. I followed the Inspector onto the rough wooden dais. A mass of noisy spectators settled into the shadows at the far end.

'Defendant Josua Baqu was parking his ox-cart backwards in the market-place,' explained the Inspector. 'Taxi driver, Absalomi Filaga, passed by. A collision occurred. Prosecution say that Josua was to blame.'

'Taxi?' I interjected, my bewilderment growing.

'Bicycle taxi, my lord. Three wheels and a trailer. Absalomi built it himself.'

There was a wave of laughter from the back. I turned to Josua, a muscular villager in *bula*-shirt and sunglasses.

'Are you pleading guilty?' I inquired.

'Not guilty,' he growled.

'And where is Mr Absalomi, the complainant in the matter?' I demanded.

The Inspector pointed through the open shutters. Outside, a gnarled figure was emerging from Vomo's most famous building—a circular edifice of wrought-iron design. Often mistaken by Methodist missionaries for a Catholic crypt, it was in fact a less spiritual memento of the French occupation in the nineteenth century—the sole public convenience in four thousand square miles of Oceania.

'Court *is* waiting,' I called to him. He hurried forward and was duly sworn as Prosecution Witness.

'May we have the substance of your complaint, Mr Absalomi?' I said.

'This fellow Josua, him drunk as usual,' he replied. 'Should do hard labour, pay damage, and be disqualified for life.'

'Is there any corroboration of this allegation?' I wanted to know.

Upon a signal from the Inspector, Absalomi produced what looked like a number plate from under his skirt. It was inscribed in great letters VOMO 1, and was heavily dented in the middle.

I turned to the defendant.

'Do you wish to cross-examine Mr Absalomi?' I asked him.

Josua shook his head, then conferred loudly with the Inspector in the local dialect.

'Defendant says he's no longer speaking to Absalomi,' the Inspector translated, 'but he does wish to call certain evidence.'

'Is the defence witness there?' I called to the back of the court. There was an extraordinary sound from the doorway.

'MOOOAH!'

A large hump-backed shape emerged from the shadows. Josua introduced me to the largest ox I had ever seen.

'*Tua-Vako-Nu*,' he said, 'Mighty Father of the Herd.'

'Testimony of this kind is totally worthless,' I told him, 'the Criminal Procedure Code makes no reference to animals.'

Josua indicated the wooden cart which was attached to the beast.

'My proof,' he declared.

I watched in dismay as he went over and unhitched the creature.

'Come closer, sir.'

'Oh, very well,' I sighed.

I walked over, intending to examine the splintered shaft. Mighty Father was barring the way, fixing me with a gloomy gaze. I squeezed past his right flank.

'This old man Absalomi,' said Josua, 'he reverse into me. Hitting here.'

I bent to make a closer inspection of the point of impact. While doing so, I received a sharp nudge in the rear. Mighty Father had consolidated his position and was now standing four square in the well of the court. Voices were raised among the spectators as they tried to cajole him to one side. For some reason he seemed attracted to the Bench. He lumbered towards it, but I got there first, by a short head.

'Interference with the course of justice is not going to be tolerated,' I ruled as I sat down, breathing hard. There were mutterings of approval from the public. I turned to my papers. The best way to cope with the situation, I decided, was to ignore it.

'It is the duty of a driver when reversing his vehicle to consult his rear-view mirror,' I pronounced. 'Did you do that, Mr Absalomi?'

'My taxi,' he countered, 'only go forwards.'

'I am merely citing the Highway Code,' I said.

I was interrupted by a loud crunching noise. I glanced over my shoulder. Mighty Father was now deep into my rucksack. I got up and advanced towards the bovine intruder, holding out a cough lozenge. My plan was to entice him quietly through the door, using the traditional British tact with animals.

'Here, boy,' I said. He pawed the floor-boards for a moment, then lowered his head.

'Watch the horns, lordship,' cried the Inspector from the safety of the witness stand.

Everyone else had retreated to the walls. Too late, I

realised the focus of the creature's gaze. A judge's red robe was not the ideal dress for this sort of confrontation.

Unfortunately I was only wearing a pair of khaki shorts beneath—my usual practice in the hot season. However, it was not the time to stand on ceremony.

Strange how the brain grows icy in a crisis, I thought.

The pages of Hemingway flashed before me as I flung off the scarlet and held it out before the enraged quadruped.

He dived towards it. I sidestepped nimbly. The roar from the gallery surged in my ears. Mighty Father missed me by inches.

Carried away, I attempted a sort of matador's double-stamp—for which, strangely enough, judicial buckle-shoes are well suited. It was enough to divert my opponent. Lowering his horns he caught up the robe and tossed it over the verandah. The next minute he had disappeared after it.

It was never seen again. I delivered a speedy verdict of acquittal and adjourned to my cabin on the Government Launch. This time I was able to make use of the skipper's radio-telephone.

'Oh, it's you again,' exclaimed Sir Neville Gawsby, when his secretary finally tracked him down for me.

' 'Fraid I've lost my robes altogether, CJ,' I said.

'How do you mean?'

'I-er-got into a sort of bull-fight, sir. Hello? Hello? Can you hear me, Sir Neville?'

'I can hear you,' he replied faintly, 'but I don't pretend to understand you.'

'It all began over a case of careless driving,' I started to explain.

'Please don't go on,' he interrupted. 'I'm washing my hands of all your inadequacies in the matter of Court Regalia.'

'But I should like you to know exactly why,' I tried again.

'No!' the Chief Justice snapped. 'Merely remember that from now on you'll be paddling your own damn canoe.'

That strangely enough, was what I was about to do.

30

Complications Set In

I was on Fandi again, in North Western Micronesia. I had
not long sent the jury out. The twelve good men and true,
ceremonially oiled and garlanded, were considering their
verdict on the verandah at the back of the Village Meeting
House. Suddenly the Registrar—it was Winston Moko
again—popped his head through the mosquito net
at the entrance to the little tent which comprised my
chambers.

'The Jury have a request to make,' he announced. 'Sitting
has to be resumed.'

I put away my nasal syringe—Dr Page Harker's Inflatable
Model for Use in the Tropics—which accompanied me on
all my judicial travels.

'Very well, Mr Moko,' I sighed. I collected my notes of
evidence together. 'Now where have you put my court
spectacles?' I demanded.

'They're on your lordship's nose,' he replied.

My chronic sinus trouble was beginning to make me
absent-minded.

I resumed my seat on the Bench, a rickety canvas chair in
faded stripes of red, white and blue, and tried to concentrate
my thoughts on the trial in progress. It was an unusual case
of abduction. The scene of the alleged crime was a cave on a
neighbouring atoll. According to the testimony of Chief
Mosese, his daughter had been lured there, against her
will, by the son of a local elder.

The youth now sat, with bent head, in the dock, his fate
in the hands of the Jury. The villagers settled down again in

packed rows on mats at the back of the court. I gave up trying to trap a particularly savage mosquito between the pages of Phipson on *Evidence*, as the Jury filed in.

'Kindly be upstanding,' I told the Foreman, a massive islander with a shaved head and boar-tusk earrings. 'What exactly is the problem?'

The Registrar stepped forward as interpreter. He spoke impeccable English—with only the slightest hint of his half-Chinese ancestry.

'It's about the cave,' reported Winston Moko. 'According to the victim's father, she was detained there by this young man without her consent.'

The defendant shook his head and shot a meaningful glance at the pretty girl in question—now sitting primly at Chief Mosese's side.

'It so happens,' the Registrar continued, 'two of the Jury are fishermen who know this cave well.' Mr Moko paused to liven up the punkah boy. There was a swish of hot air as the canvas flaps rattled into motion.

'These jurors insist,' the Registrar continued, 'it is not an ordinary cave. There are so many ways out that nobody could be kept there who wanted to run away.'

This was manifestly a crucial point!

'The court will inspect the *locus in quo*,' I decreed.

I stood up and gave a slightly twisted bow, precipitated by the punkah now in violent action above my head. I joined the Registrar on the way out of court.

'How far is this place, exactly?' I asked him.

He pointed through the wooden shutters across the lagoon. 'No distance,' he indicated.

There was only time for a snack in chambers—a rather green banana and a tot of mango juice—before Mr Moko reported back.

'All ready,' he said, leading the way down to the beach. He had obtained the largest outrigger canoe available. One by one the twelve stout gentlemen of the Jury clambered aboard.

'A bit of a squeeze,' I chaffed, tugging my gown from beneath the Foreman's grass skirt.

Winston Moko jerked the 'put-put' engine into action and away we glided.

Once beyond the reef, I joined him by the tiller.

'Regarding this development in the case,' I began, 'did you have time to check what the Noumoan Criminal Procedure code has to say as to the rights of the accused?'

He seemed too preoccupied by the huge waves now breaking over us to reply. No doubt our native craft was designed to travel pretty low in the sea.

'At present, of course,' I continued, 'it may be simply a question of bail.'

Something like a smile flickered over Mr Moko's oriental features.

'In more ways than one, sir,' he replied, indicating the rising water around our ankles.

The next moment, the ever-resourceful Registrar was handing me a coconut shell from under the seat.

'Quick thinking,' I had to agree, as he distributed similar containers to the Jury. 'Bale away, gentlemen,' I said.

We never did make the atoll. For safety's sake, a swift return to base was necessary. Fortunately, on the way back, Chief Mosese had a brief word in Mr Moko's ear.

'It seems the Chief has changed his mind,' the Registrar informed me. 'He no longer wishes to press the charge.'

He glanced towards the twelve portly jurors.

'Decided on the weight of the evidence, you might say, my lord.'

My final port of call, on that particular Assize-Circuit, was Faya, a tiny atoll to the east of Fandi. Court was a simple enough affair. Just my canvas chair and folding table under a coconut tree.

The solitary case in the List was a domestic dispute involving the light-house keeper and his wife, sole inhabitants of the place. Neither party turned up, however. In fact there was no sign of anybody.

'Case dismissed,' I was saying, more or less to myself, when I heard the sound of a large motor-cruiser coming ashore.

A party of trippers, from the mainland, landed on the beach beside me. Jolly shouts and cries accompanied the usual clicking of cameras. I looked up to find myself the object of considerable interest.

'He must be what they call a beachcomber,' said an elderly English lady tourist to her companion. 'The Guide Book says they've died out.'

I suppose my appearance was a bit informal, now that I was without the distinctive cover of the red gown. I had kicked off my sandals in the heat, and had on a rather worn pair of white ducks. Even so, it was a nasty shock to hear myself described in that way.

'Mr Solomoni!' I called in what I hoped was a voice of authority.

The portly form of my orderly surfaced from behind a sand-dune, where he had been attending to a call of nature.

'The business of the Supreme Court appears to be over. Kindly row me back to the Government Launch.'

The visitors broke ranks in puzzled silence as I stalked through, followed by Mr Solomoni, carrying my chair and table.

'Good-day to you all,' I said, with a curt bow, before taking my seat in the dinghy, where the orderly took up the oars.

Were my standards of judicial dress beginning to slip? I wondered, on the voyage back to Fulala.

To be on the safe side, I instructed the Fulala tailor to run up something more formal for court wear. After several conferences in his dimly-lit hut on the corner of the market-place, the Judge's Suit was delivered to my chambers, wrapped in a piece of barkcloth. It was intended to be a tropical version of the English barrister's dark dress, but in the bright sunlight of the South Pacific, the black alpaca chosen by the island tailor had an ominous gleam. It shone like gravestone marble. The shoulders, too, were oddly rucked, giving an almost hunchback effect.

On the day when I tried it out on the Bench, I was still wearing a black eye-patch because of an infection caught from a sand-fly on Faya. The defendant, a tiny Bokoan, charged with an Immigration Offence, took one look at me and dived out of the dock. In a flash, before the warder could grab him, he was out on the verandah and plunging down into the shark-infested water of the lagoon. Surrounded by an anxious staff, I watched him bob slowly across the waves, making for the far side of the bay at least a mile away. A police boat followed in hot pursuit, and he wa soon brought back by the warder, forlorn and dripping in the dock.

'Prisoner has to be deported,' explained the Prosecuting Inspector. I made the necessary order.

'He'll need a change of clothing for the journey,' I pointed out. I adjourned eagerly to chambers.

Rumour has it that the suit now decorates the Ancestral Mummy in the spirit-temple of Waiwaizam-Boko.

I always intended to call and pay my respects, when next on circuit in the area, but that was not to be.

31

Full Circle

'You'd better get up to a hill station for local leave,' advised the Fulala Medical Officer. Further loss of weight had led me to consult him, and I was finding the coastal humidity of the island capital more taxing that season than usual. 'Get some fresh air into your lungs,' he added, 'and try to eat some decent meals.'

Icy rain was thundering down on the tin roof of the Attabhoi Guest House as I paid off my taxi-driver and checked in. The Attabhoi, a modest hostelry with decaying shutters, suited my purse rather better than the fashionable hotel on the other side of the mountain.

'It's certainly bracing up here,' I enthused to the decrepit bearer who shuffled me into my little windswept bower at the end of the north-east verandah. The poor fellow's teeth were chattering too much to allow him to reply.

It was still raining heavily when I joined Mr Attabhoi, mine host, at the festive board.

'How long do these storms usually last?' I inquired.

'Maybe three, maybe four weeks,' he replied.

Mr Attabhoi was a retired schoolmaster. I gathered from his heavy breathing during mastication that he practised yoga. The menu was strictly vegetarian.

'Feed the soul,' said Mr Attabhoi, spearing a curried bean with his fork, 'the flesh, it is to be despised.' The mosquitoes that night thought otherwise. They kept up a constant attack upon me while I was trying to work upon some reserved judgements. Eventually my lamp ran out of kerosene so I retreated to bed under the mosquito net.

'Do you have any insecticide in the house?' I asked Mr.

Attabhoi at breakfast next morning. Removing my plimsoll I indicated a constellation of mosquito bites upon the instep. Mr Attabhoi fixed me with his mad burning eyes.

'I am never permitting the slaughter of life,' he decreed. This became very apparent. Indeed, the scuttling of the cockroaches in my chamber that evening gave me another sleepless night. At dawn I surveyed my waxen features in the cracked mirror of Mr Attabhoi's Gothic bathroom.

'Hang the expense,' I resolved, 'might as well live it up at the hotel.' As a measure of economy I decided to get there by the local bus. Mr Attabhoi packed me a curry bean sandwich with a resigned air and directed me to the terminal.

'Thunder an Lightning Transport Service,' read the giant mauve letters across the windscreen of the omnibus. 'Proprietor', continued the inscription, 'J. NAM (deceased)'. The last word was in sepia. It had been added, I assumed, by the young man who sat on the ancient bonnet chewing a stick of sugar cane. This was the loyal son of the late Mr Nam.

'All aboard,' he shouted, springing unexpectedly at the controls. There were no doors or windows in the vehicle. Clouds of dust from the mountain track swirled in as we hurtled alongside the ravine. At one point a Parsee gentleman in black coat and white leggings leapt aboard. Blinded by the dust of the interior, he seated himself, short-sightedly, upon my lap.

'Afraid this seat's taken,' I called down his ear.

It was something of a relief to find myself, some minutes later, deposited with my set of law books and case files outside the hotel.

After the Attabhoi, the luxury of the place seemed exhilarating. There was even a swimming pool.

Why not take a dip? I thought. Give me an appetite for lunch.

The hotel was full of ANZAC army officers on a climbing expedition. Great tanned fellows, I gave them a sociable 'good morning' as I emerged from the bathing hut. 'Some people have the decency to keep their skeletons in the cupboard,' observed one of them waggishly over his beer.

My days in the tropics had by no means made me into a strong swimmer, but my breast-cum-side stroke did now get me along, albeit in a diagonal direction. Too late, I realised why my fellow guests had not joined me in a dip. At that time of the year the altitude made the temperature of the water uncomfortably low. By the time cramp drove me out of the pool it was already apparent that I was developing some sort of Polynesian Croup.

'The last straw,' said the Medical Officer, when I reported back to him. He totted up the list of my various tropical complaints and sent me home to the Westminster School of Tropical Medicine.

'This time, old chap,' Mr Bottomley enthused, shortly after my arrival, 'your ailments are absolutely genuine.' He sat down excitedly on the bed, before I had time to remove my left foot. The Consultant was noticeably heavier than at our last meeting in the Westminster School of Tropical Medicine.

'Never seen such a collection of wildlife in a single blood-specimen,' he beamed. 'A walking aquarium, you might say.' He handed my lab-report back to Sister. 'Take care of that,' he stipulated, 'it's medical history.'

I was able to watch a complete re-run of Dr Kildare on colour TV in the Albert Schweitzer Ward, before the Consultant agreed to discharge me.

'No more of the tropics for you,' he decreed, closing the bulging flap of my case papers. 'Why not take a long holiday and write your memoirs?'

I decided to follow Mr Bottomley's advice.